Lean Human Performance Improvement

Jerry L. Harbour

CRC Press
Taylor & Francis Group
Boca Raton London New York

CRC Press is an imprint of the
Taylor & Francis Group, an **informa** business

A PRODUCTIVITY PRESS BOOK

CRC Press
Taylor & Francis Group
6000 Broken Sound Parkway NW, Suite 300
Boca Raton, FL 33487-2742

© 2015 by Taylor & Francis Group, LLC
CRC Press is an imprint of Taylor & Francis Group, an Informa business

No claim to original U.S. Government works

Printed on acid-free paper
Version Date: 20141007

International Standard Book Number-13: 978-1-4822-9881-9 (Paperback)

Library of Congress Cataloging-in-Publication Data

Harbour, Jerry L.
  Lean human performance improvement / Jerry L. Harbour.
    pages cm
  Includes bibliographical references and index.
  ISBN 978-1-4822-9881-9
  1. Performance technology. 2. Performance--Measurement. 3. Labor productivity. I. Title.

HF5549.5.P37H367 2015
658.3'14--dc23   2014024963

Visit the Taylor & Francis Web site at
http://www.taylorandfrancis.com

and the CRC Press Web site at
http://www.crcpress.com

Dedicated to my late grandfather, Clarence Nelson, who instilled in me at a very young age a love for books and learning; something that I hope my own young grandson, Caden, will inherit and nourish throughout his lifetime as well.

.

Contents

SECTION II   ANALYZING AND IMPROVING HUMAN-RELATED WORK PRODUCTIVITY

SECTION III   ANALYZING AND IMPROVING HUMAN-RELATED QUALITY AND SAFETY

Chapter 1

A Work System Perspective: People, Tools, and Tasks

Envision, if you will, a work setting. Any setting will do. It can be an operating theater in a hospital, an assembly line at an auto plant, a regional distribution center, or an aircraft maintenance facility at a major airport. What do you picture?

Individually, our descriptions of those settings probably would vary widely, one from another. But, when taken collectively, a common theme likely would emerge, and that theme almost certainly would entail people (whom we generally call workers) using tools and other forms of technology to perform a myriad of different work-related tasks. This people–tools–tasks triad forms the beginning components of a very simple work system model that I have illustrated in Figure 1.1. I could certainly expand the depicted model, making it much more complex. However, for now, let's keep it simple, using just people, tools, and tasks.

Unfortunately, in our quest to improve a work system, we oftentimes focus only on the technology and/or task parts of the formula, sometimes forgetting the human element altogether. Technologists, for example, attempt to improve the tools part of the formula. Lean Six Sigma practitioners focus mostly on the task and associated process part. Yet, this myopic approach to work system improvement often leads to unusable and confusing technologies, and human unfriendly and inefficient work processes. If we are to significantly improve any work system, regardless

Figure 1.1   Three-component work system model.

of a specific setting, then we must focus our efforts not only on all of the individual elements comprising the system—the people, tools, and tasks—but also on the collective interactions between and among those system elements.

This holistic and interactive insight into work system improvement is certainly nothing new or revolutionary. In fact, it is over a century old, forming the very basis of Frank Gilbreth's (1868–1924) pioneering work improvement methods.

As described by Yost (1949), in the late 1800s, Gilbreth began an apprenticeship as a young bricklayer. During the course of his apprenticeship, he worked under several different master bricklayers, each one teaching him a different bricklaying technique. Being naturally curious, Gilbreth began to consider how best to accomplish the task of laying bricks in the most efficient and effective manner possible.

Transforming this curiosity into a lifelong study of work improvement, Gilbreth started his own construction business in 1895 at the age of 27. He was aided in this endeavor by his wife, Lillian Evelyn Moller Gilbreth, who was one of the first working female engineers to hold a PhD. She also is recognized by many historians as the first true industrial and organizational psychologist in the United States. The Gilbreth-founded company specialized in "speed building" or building brick buildings faster and better than anyone else. Under Gilbreth's guidance, his company rapidly became one of the largest construction firms operating on the East Coast.

The company's success at speed building is best illustrated by the construction of the Lowell Laboratory at the Massachusetts Institute of Technology. Gilbreth's company completed building the Lowell Laboratory less than three months after signing the initial contract. This feat was accomplished despite the fact that the project was delayed at the outset for 10 days due to heavy rains. As described in the *Boston Evening Transcript*:

> … thirteen hundred piles had been driven, a million bricks laid, iron beams placed and concrete foundations strong enough to support heavy engines and dynamos, and an adequate heating and ventilating system installed—forty thousand square feet laid out in forty-seven rooms, and a power house besides.

Perhaps even more impressive than the actual accomplishment was Gilbreth's method for achieving it. Gilbreth would study each construction job in order to identify wasted human motion and effort. Then he would redesign the work and develop supporting technologies, making the job for his workers as simple, efficient, and easy as possible. This systematic approach to work design is best illustrated in the area of bricklaying.

After studying the bricklaying process, Gilbreth was able to reduce the number of motions required to lay a single brick from 18 to 4.5 (the half motion being shared with laying the next brick). This remarkable time savings was brought about by identifying and then eliminating wasted motions and steps associated with the laying of each brick, rearranging the placement of the bricks and mortar to a more accessible and easily reachable location, and redesigning the scaffolding to increase bricklaying speed and reduce worker fatigue.

As a result of these changes, Gilbreth's bricklayers could lay some 350 bricks per hour, nearly tripling the previous record of 120 bricks per hour. In fact, his bricklayers averaged laying 2,600 bricks per day as opposed to the industry's working average of 500 bricks per day.

Note how Gilbreth focused first and foremost on his bricklayers, his workers, to make their work faster, simpler, and less fatiguing. But, of equal importance, this focus included an analysis and improvement of the tasks, supported by a redesign of supporting technologies (i.e., the scaffolding). In essence, Gilbreth significantly increased worker output, as measured by the number of bricks laid per hour and per day, by focusing on the *total integration* of people, tools, and tasks.

Much has taken place in the work setting since Frank and Lillian Gilbreth's groundbreaking performance improvement efforts some 100 years ago. Yet, as evidenced by today's many Lean Six Sigma initiatives, businesses and industries alike are still very much interested in improving work performance and increasing worker productivity and the quality of that work. Although work settings may have changed over the years, and fewer of us now lay bricks for a living, the basic concepts of work improvement as outlined by Frank and Lillian Gilbreth have stayed remarkably the same.

Therefore, as companies continue their endeavors to improve work performance, they must ensure that their ongoing "leaning" activities include a healthy appreciation for, and recognition of, human performance. For, despite increasing technologically sophisticated work systems, those systems are still designed, built, maintained, and operated by us, sometimes fallible, humans. Ignoring the human component of work performance is at best a recipe for unnecessary waste, inefficiency, and decreased productivity. At worst, it can spell disaster.

Human Work Performance

This book is primarily about human performance in the workplace, its analysis and subsequent improvement, something that I euphemistically term *Lean Human Performance Improvement*. Yet, a basic underlying precept of Lean human performance improvement is that humans can never be fully divorced from the tasks they are performing or the tools they are using to perform those tasks. In many instances, it is those very same tasks and tools that are at the very root of human performance problems.

Following World War II, for example, it was discovered that in the U.S. Army Air Force alone, some 15,000 service personnel died in training and other related aircraft incidents while flying in the United States. This tragic figure represented approximately one third of the 62,500 army air force aircraft lost during the entire war effort. The primary cause listed for most of these training fatalities was simply "pilot error."

In an attempt to better understand pilot error, Paul Fitts (1912–1965), a psychologist at Ohio State University, who served in the air force as a lieutenant colonel, undertook an extensive analysis of all aircraft training-related fatalities that occurred during the war. He was aided in this effort by R. E. Jones.

The two investigators quickly discovered that features of World War II airplane cockpits systematically influenced the way in which pilots made errors. For example, pilots often confused flap and landing gear handles. The two handles typically looked and felt the same, and were co-located next to each other. This confusing handle resemblance and dual placement sometimes resulted in pilots inadvertently changing flap positions when they intended only to lower or raise the landing gear, a mistake that on occasion proved fatal.

Pilots also mixed up the locations of throttle, mixture, and propeller controls. The placement and order of these controls kept changing across different cockpits and airplane models. Imagine if auto manufacturers today placed the gas pedal to the right of the brake in some of their models and to the left of the brake in other models. If you mistakenly stepped on the gas when attempting to slam on the brakes in your rental vehicle, causing an accident, would this really be a case of human or driver error? Most of us would not think so and neither did Fitts and Jones.

Summarizing their findings in a seminal article published in 1949, the two investigators concluded that the term "pilot error" was deemed unsatisfactory. It should be used only as an initial pointer in hunting for deeper, more systematic conditions that can lead to failure. Observing that human error is often connected to features of people's tools and tasks, they argued that we can retool and redesign work settings, thus positively influencing the way in which people perform tasks—this all in 1949.

Thanks to the initial work of Fitts and Jones, and many other investigators since then, the aviation industry, both commercial and military, has come a long way in continuously improving their flight safety records. This does not mean, however, that critical lessons learned years ago are not sometimes forgotten.

For example, the Predator drone was originally developed as an unmanned aerial reconnaissance vehicle. The Predator is remotely piloted from ground control stations located hundreds and even thousands of miles away by bouncing signals off of satellites. In 2001, it was armed with Hellfire air-to-ground missiles. Unfortunately in earlier modeled ground control stations, the button used to launch the deadly Hellfire missiles was located only a quarter of an inch away from the button that was used to kill the Predator's engine. This illogical dual-button placement created an obvious error-prone situation with potentially deadly consequences. According to author Mark Mazzetti (2013), pilots likened the haphazard layout of early Predator flight control panels to the "… scattered features of a Mr. Potato Head doll."

Like the aviation industry, many other industries struggle with human error in the workplace. The medical industry, for example, continues to deal with human error, especially potentially catastrophic errors that take place during surgery and in intensive care units. Surgeons not only sometimes mistakenly leave items in patients, but they even on occasion operate on (or worse yet, remove) the wrong body part, which *was* perfectly healthy prior to its removal.

The oil industry is no different. Following the explosion, fire, sinking, and subsequent oil spill from the drilling rig *Deepwater Horizon* in the Gulf of Mexico, numerous accident investigations were conducted and resultant findings published. One investigative report concluded that, "The drilling crew and other individuals on the rig also missed critical signs that a kick was occurring. The crew could have prevented the blowout—or at least significantly reduced its impact—if they had reacted in a timely and appropriate manner."

Although this finding seems to squarely place blame on the actions of the rig crew itself, there is no deeper analysis in the report to assess whether these missed critical signals were actually displayed to rig personnel and in what manner. If displayed, could they easily have been detected and clearly understood in a very noisy, dirty, and busy work environment? And, if detected and understood, was there sufficient time to react in a "timely and appropriate manner?"

If we are to truly improve work performance, making it more productive, reliable, and safer, then we must go beyond the overused designation of human error and our often kneejerk reaction to shaming, blaming, and punishing the offending error-producing parties. Rather, we must dig deeper to better understand the why and how behind such errors.

Book Overview

Lean Human Performance Improvement consists of three major parts:

    I. Understanding human performance
    II. Analyzing and improving work productivity
   III. Analyzing and improving quality and safety

The goal of Part I is to first develop a fundamental and basic understanding of human performance, then couple that understanding with learning how to analyze and improve human-related work productivity (Part II), and quality and safety (Part III). The good news is that, although used tools and tasks may vary widely from one work setting to another, the human subsystem stays much the same. Accordingly, there is a great deal of applicability and transfer from one work environment to another. Thus, lessons learned in work setting A have considerable application to work setting B, even if the two settings differ widely in function and character.

The initial "understanding" human performance Part I section consists of Chapters 2 through 4. Chapter 2 (A Macro Model: Nature, Nurture, and Operational Setting) and Chapter 3 (A Micro Model: Perception, Cognition, and Action) present two basic models of human performance, first at the macro level and then at the more detailed, individual micro level. The two presented models incorporate both a psychological *and* biological view of human performance. These two somewhat differing views are both needed if we are to truly understand many of the underlying tenets of human performance, or how and why humans perform the way that they do.

A *model* represents nothing more than a tentative description of a system that attempts to account for many of its properties. A well-developed model can facilitate the understanding of how a system (e.g., a human) works and perhaps, more importantly, provide practical insight into how to improve that system (my ultimate goal here).

Unfortunately, many models of human performance are developed and described through the lens of a single discipline or a specific area of interest. Important insights gained from modeling athletic sports performance, for example, are rarely incorporated into more cognitive-centric models developed for describing work performance. Consequently, there is often a disproportionate emphasis and bias on understanding and improving cognitive or mental skills in the workplace at the almost total neglect of understanding and improving motor or physical skills. (This same narrow sightedness happened in my own human performance-related PhD program.)

Additionally, critical insights gained from industry X (e.g., aviation) are mistakenly thought to have little, if any, direct application to industry Y (e.g., medical). However, if we are to better understand and improve human performance, then we must incorporate and integrate diverse findings from a broad spectrum of human performance-related fields and across varied industrial work settings. This is something that I attempt to do in Chapters 2 and 3, as well as throughout the rest of the book.

Further, the focus of Chapters 2 and 3 is primarily on individual performance. Although work performance is often a function of team performance, the basic unit of team performance is still individual performance. In many instances, team performance is simply an extension of highly choreographed, collective individual performances. Accordingly, it is this individual level that represents our initial starting point for understanding human performance and is the primary focus throughout *Lean Human Performance Improvement*.

Chapters 2 and 3 also point out the sometimes harsh reality of human performance variability or differences between and among individual performers. In some instances, especially with simple tasks, large initial differences in performance can be significantly (but not always completely) mitigated with training and practice.

For example, following the theft of Leonardo Da Vinci's *Mona Lisa* from the Louvre Museum in Paris on an August morning in 1911, French police detectives set up an interesting and insightful reconstruction of the robbery. Several male volunteers were enlisted as would-be thieves to reenact the crime. Each volunteer had to steal a fake *Mona Lisa* painting hanging in the exact same configuration as the real painting as quickly as possible. The make-believe thieves, however, were unaware of how the picture was actually hung. As a result of this lack of knowledge and having never practiced the task before, the volunteer thieves took at least five minutes to remove the painting, all experiencing great difficulty in the process.

By comparison, experienced Louvre staff members expertly lifted and detached the fake *Mona Lisa* painting from its four supporting hooks in some six seconds. In this example, such wide gaps in human performance levels would almost certainly have been ameliorated, most likely significantly so, if the make-believe thieves had received training and practice in removing the painting prior to the beginning of the exercise.[*]

In other instances, however, and even with the exact same type and length of training and associated practice, a *divergence* in performance levels may occur among individuals. This observation seems especially true with difficult tasks. In these more difficult task instances, the actual "trainability" of an individual often becomes a critical differentiator in determining subsequently achieved task performance levels.

One possible explanation for these observed differences in human trainability is a person's "nature" or unique genotype biology. This observation is particularly evident in sport settings, but may be a requirement in almost any work setting as well. Surgeons, for example, may be naturally endowed with superior eye–hand coordination. This pretraining genetic endowment may allow them to more easily master the techniques of surgery, especially the more difficult physical motor components. It is hard to even imagine a brain surgeon, at least a successful one, having lousy eye–hand coordination.

---

[*] The painting was recovered in Milan, Italy, in December 1913, from an Italian who had worked at the Louvre and taken the *Mona Lisa* so that it could be returned to his country after being stolen by Napoleon.

In some instances, such requisite and unique genetic endowments can be measured rather precisely. For example, Leonardo da Vinci's famous *Vitruvian Man* has an arm span equal to his height, representing a perfect ratio of 1.0. Most people have this same perfect 1.0 ratio. However, there are some interesting exceptions. National Basketball Association (NBA) players have an average arm-span-to-height-ratio of 1.063. This means that an average-height NBA player of 6'7" has a wingspan of 7 feet. David Epstein, author of *The Sports Gene* (2013), notes that not only are NBA players "… outlandishly tall, they also are preposterously long, even relative to their stature."

By comparison, Olympic-caliber weightlifters are relatively short in height and ideally have arm-span-to-height-ratios of less than 1.0. All else being equal, weightlifters with shorter arms, and especially shorter forearms, have a significant advantage over their longer arm opponents in that they literally do not have to lift the heavy weights overhead as far. In this weightlifting task-specific example, shorter arms are an advantage whereas in basketball, they are a distinct disadvantage. Also note that arm span is genetically or biologically controlled. That is, one really cannot train to have longer or shorter arms, no matter how much someone might try.

It is perhaps a good thing that da Vinci did not use NBA players or Olympic weightlifters as models for his *Vitruvian Man*. If he had, his perfectly proportional square and circle would have had to have been replaced by a lop-sided rectangle and ellipse, negating the painting's flawless symmetry.

Chapter 4, entitled Human Error (Or Is It Really?), introduces various types of human errors and their associated precursors (called *error-producing conditions*). The chapter further describes where human errors may occur in a particular task sequence—representing so-called error-prone activities—and why. For example, surgeons forgetting to remove a surgical sponge following an operation and electricians failing to remove grounding plugs prior to reenergizing a newly installed transformer at first may seem to represent very different error occurrences. Yet, both errors represent the same error type (errors of omission) and both errors occur in almost the exact same location in the overall task sequence. As such, learning about human error in one work setting has a great deal of applicability and transfer to other seemingly dissimilar settings.

Additionally, and as illustrated in the World War II pilot error study, embedded features in a system, termed *latent factors* or *errors*, often "set up" consequent human or active errors. One way, therefore, to reduce the adverse consequences of human error is to remove latent factors from a work system (somewhat akin to removing potential landmines), thus making the system more human friendly and error tolerant.

As described by Harbour (2009a) and graphically illustrated in Figure 1.2, work organizations often have dual goals. One goal is to enhance success space via accruing increases in work efficiency and productivity. Another goal is to avoid, or at least significantly diminish, costly ventures into failure space by decreasing unwanted incident frequency and associated consequence severity. Thus, armed with a basic understanding about human performance developed in Part I, Part II focuses on the productivity part of the organizational success goal depicted in Figure 1.2. Part III takes on the failure space portion of the figure. If we stop to think about it, most Lean Six Sigma improvement efforts also focus simultaneously on improving work productivity and work quality, as well as safety.

It is always important to realize, however, that improving work productivity *and* work reliability can never be completely divorced one from the other. For example, removing wasted and unnecessary human motions can certainly improve the speed of work. However, if quality-related errors are still being made in this more streamlined process version, necessitating rework, then those initial time savings and associated increases in work productivity are instantly negated. Additionally, if a severe accident occurs, then work is often stopped completely. Accordingly, we must always think about productivity *and* quality *and* safety when trying to improve overall work performance.

Fiction writers Preston and Child (2014) capture this integrated need perfectly when they note that it isn't enough to "figure out how to do something right. You also have to figure out how *not* to do something wrong. You have to analyze every possible path to failure. Only then can you be sure of success."

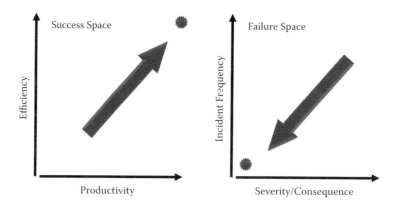

Figure 1.2 Organizational goals regarding success and failure space.

Part II consists of Chapters 5 and 6. Chapter 5 (Human Motion Analysis) describes various techniques that are applicable in analyzing human performance from a work productivity viewpoint, thus making work efforts faster and easier. The analytical techniques presented in Chapter 5 focus primarily on the identification of waste in the form of nonvalue-adding human motions and associated individual task steps. Described analytical techniques in Chapter 5 include some of the very same types of analyses that allowed Frank Gilbreth to reduce the number of required motions in laying a single brick from 18 to 4.5.

Because most human work is accomplished by using our hands, Chapter 5 also includes a detailed section on analyzing hand motions. A hand-related motion analysis is something that Frank Gilbreth labeled *therblig analysis* and is, today, often referred to as a hand micromotion analysis.

One aspect of Chapter 5 that may be a bit different for the Lean Six Sigma practitioner is the emphasis on saving literally seconds and minutes. Because many human motions are repeated over and over again in the workplace, microsavings of even a few seconds can often aggregate into significant savings at the macro level. For example, Gilbreth saved some 46 seconds in the laying of each brick. Yet, this seemingly minor individual savings translated into a huge macrosaving as measured by the number of bricks that could be laid in a single hour or day. As described in Chapter 5, in order to accrue such microsavings requires modeling and analyzing human performance at a very detailed, almost microscopic level.

Once work-related human motions have been analyzed and specific areas for improvement have been identified, the next step is developing and implementing those improvement methods. Chapter 6, titled Human Productivity Improvement, addresses this next improvement development and implementation phase.

One aspect of Chapter 6 focuses on some of the specifics of work setting design or layout, especially from a human performance "motion" improvement perspective. Other sections describe how to eliminate or at least significantly reduce unnecessary and nonvalue-adding human motions in a task sequence. In many instances and as described in Chapter 6, a redesigned work setting can lead to reducing or eliminating unnecessary and wasted human motions. In other instances, redesigning a task sequence can accomplish the same thing. As described in both Chapters 5 and 6, an overall human motion-related improvement strategy is to think micro small and save macro big.

Part III is comprised of Chapters 7 and 8. Chapter 7 (Human Error Analysis) focuses on analyzing human performance from a human error perspective, with the end goal of making human performance more reliable (and, thus, less error prone). Whether analyzing a vexing and persistent quality problem, or investigating a serious accident, the techniques presented in Chapter 7 work equally well. Of special importance in such investigative circumstances is the need to become "one with the human performer." That is, by looking at a situation from the perspective of the individual who committed the error. As such, this looking from the "inside out" should always be a critical component of any adverse incident analysis.

As described by Sidney Dekker (2002), "people's behavior is rational, if possibly erroneous, when viewed from the inside of their situations, not from the outside and from hindsight." According to Dekker, the point in learning about human error is "… not to find out where people went wrong. It is to find out why their assessments and actions made sense to them at the time, given how their situation looked from the inside." As described in Chapter 7, adapting Dekker's "looking from the inside out" approach to analyzing human performance problems can provide valuable insights, not only as to why an unwanted event may have occurred, but, more importantly, how to possibly prevent its reoccurrence.

Chapter 8 (Human Quality and Safety Improvement) provides various techniques into improving task reliability and related work quality and safety performance. The chapter describes a number of human error reduction methods, such as providing good reminders and other types of job aids that can improve cognition, especially remembering. Chapter 8 further describes how some of the techniques and concepts of poka-yoke or mistake-proofing can be applied to improving work quality and safety. In a poka-yoke system, the emphasis is not so much on the reduction of errors per se, but rather on the elimination of the "consequences" associated with making those errors. Further, the critical role of enhancing perception is discussed. In some work settings, poor visual displays can negatively affect human understanding, which, in turn, can sometimes lead to unintended errors. Unfortunately, humans cannot mentally process or understand something that they cannot first detect or sense.

Chapter 9 (And That's It) provides a final summary of critical takeaway points made in all previous chapters. An extended glossary and reference list are also located at the end of the book. Not knowing the reader's level of familiarity with this human performance subject, I attempted to make the glossary especially comprehensive.

All chapters contain multiple examples from diverse work settings to explain key points. Major case studies also are included in some chapters. The goal of all included examples and case studies is to develop a generic understanding that, in turn, can be successfully applied to any work setting. And, as described, that basic understanding must always center on a synergistic appreciation of people, tools, and tasks; something that Frank and Lillian Gilbreth understood more than 100 years ago and something that has not really changed that much since those initial, ground-breaking efforts.

In summary, *Lean Human Performance Improvement* attempts to present a broad overview of human performance in the workplace. My goal in writing this book is primarily to assist Lean Six Sigma team members in better understanding how humans can positively and negatively affect work performance. A secondary goal is to provide a more comprehensive introductory treatment of human performance for the applied human performance improvement practitioner. If I have succeeded in some small way in achieving either of these dual goals, then the effort has definitely been worthwhile. So, as always, please enjoy.

UNDERSTANDING HUMAN PERFORMANCE

1

If the brain were so simple we could understand it, we would be so simple we couldn't.

—Chinese Fortune Cookie

Chapter 2

A Macro Model: Nature, Nurture, and Operational Setting

Working for a private company, I once served as the director of training at a federal government agency-owned national training center. Federal government employees oversaw the center, while the company that I worked for was responsible for developing and conducting all training, as well as performing all other related support and operational activities.

The center specialized in safety, security, and protective force training. It had an especially robust protective force training program. To support this training specialty, the center had multiple onsite shooting ranges of differing distances and a so-called "shoot house" where trainees could practice room-clearing and other tactical operations in a safe and controlled environment.

Protective force training courses ranged from basic to highly advanced. They lasted in duration anywhere from a few days to multiple weeks. One advanced course offered by the center, which was especially challenging, was called Tactical Response Force or TRF training. The multiweek training session was somewhat akin to an extended SWAT-type course, except on steroids. Or as one trainee once said, "… it's nothing but six weeks of runnin' and gunnin'."

Successful completion and certification of TRF normally meant a promotion and associated pay raise back at the trainee's home worksite. As such, students were highly motivated to succeed in the course. Being selected to attend TRF training was considered a real honor and privilege.

Yet, passing TRF was not easy. At the end of each week's training module, a demanding skill-based performance test was administered. Particularly challenging was the obstacle or "O" course test administered approximately halfway through the course. If trainees should fail an individual performance test, they were given a second chance to pass. Unfortunately, a second failure meant automatic dismissal from the course, necessitating the trainee returning to his (almost all trainees were males) home site without earning the coveted TRF certification.

We once unintentionally ran an extremely insightful experiment regarding TRF training and the vagaries of human performance, in general. Due to scheduling considerations and course demand, we had to run two TRF courses congruently, with only a one-week break in between. Because of this back-to-back scheduling need, everything was essentially the same between the two courses: the exact same curriculum, testing, equipment, environmental conditions (e.g., weather), and, most importantly, the exact same set of instructors (for safety purposes, the course required a large number of lead and assistant instructors).

The only real difference between the two TRF courses was the composition of the students themselves, and that single difference literally made all of the difference in the world. In the first TRF course, most students excelled, easily passing all performance tests with flying colors. The dropout or failure rate for the first course was well below average.

In comparison, the second course's outcome was essentially the exact opposite. Numerous students failed the course and had to be sent home early, much to the angst and expense of their sponsoring home sites. Following this disastrous second TRF course session, some training center government officials wanted an explanation for the unusually high failure rate and, by insinuation, what we (the instructors) had done wrong.

My response to their individual queries was that our instructors had done nothing wrong. In point of fact, they had worked much harder in the second TRF course than they had in the first. I argued, therefore, that the "nurture" or training part of the nature–nurture equation was exactly the same in both courses. By contrast, the really big and marked difference between the two courses was the so-called "nature" part of the equation.

What we had unfortunately observed in the two courses was the sometimes brutal contrast in individual performance levels as a function of individual differences. Schmidt and Weinberg (2004) define *individual differences* as differences in people's performance levels that are due largely to differences in their stable and enduring abilities. In this case, it was not the training (and associated instructors) that was flawed, but rather the initial selection of personnel for the course in the first place (which was controlled by each individual home site).

As illustrated by this "unequal" training example, human performance is a complex phenomenon, often involving a multitude of highly varied and integrated factors. Many of those factors are found externally in the environments in which humans work. However, some of those factors also are internal to the individual performer him- or herself. These internal factors partially represent a biologically controlled aspect of human performance that also must be taken into consideration.

Accordingly, to begin to understand human performance, we must think of it as a veritable alphabet soup, running the gamut from A to Z. To commence our exploration of this fascinating, if not messy, alphabet soup mixture, I have chosen to present a high-level, macro model of human performance as an initial starting point. Parts of the developed model have been described earlier (Harbour, 2012).

Subsequently in Chapter 3, an accompanying micro-level model of human performance is presented (also presented in an earlier journal publication (Harbour, 2013a)). These two macro- and micro-level, model-based presentations will hopefully equip the reader with two differing, yet complimentary and somewhat overlapping views of human performance. Both models provide a great deal of information about human performance, as well as entail an initial basis for analyzing and improving human performance in the workplace, irrespective of individual work settings.

The Model

As defined in Chapter 1, a *model* represents nothing more than a tentative description of a system that attempts to account for many of its properties. The challenge in developing any model is to find the right balance between complexity and simplicity. A model that is too complex negates understanding, yet a model that is overly simplistic has little value for the applied practitioner.

The major components of the macro model that I have developed regarding human performance at the individual level are depicted in Figure 2.1. As illustrated, the developed model identifies the various properties or factors that affect some achieved or "realized" task-specific human

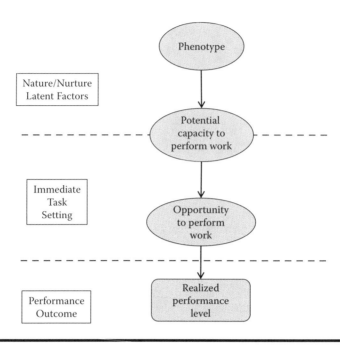

Figure 2.1   Basic components of a macro-level human performance model.

performance outcome. The depicted base model is divided into three primary, but overlapping, layers, and is comprised of:

■ a nature/nurture latent factor layer;
■ an immediate task setting layer; and
■ a performance outcome layer.

As diagrammed in Figure 2.2:

■ Nature/nurture latent factors result in a unique human phenotype that, in turn, affects a human's potential capacity to perform work. In other words, it is this unique phenotype that we *bring* to the workplace.
■ An individual's potential capacity to perform work also is affected by the immediate task setting. These task setting-related factors also affect a given opportunity to perform work.
■ Finally, nature/nurture latent factors *and* immediate task setting combine to result in some acceptable or unacceptable performance outcome.

Each major level of the model and more-detailed, associated subcomponents are explored more fully in the following sections.

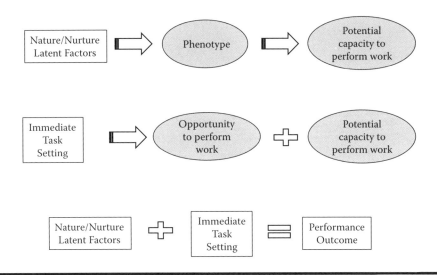

Figure 2.2 **Model component interrelationships.**

Nature/Nurture

As illustrated in Figure 2.3, an individual's potential capacity to perform work is heavily influenced by that individual's particular phenotype. In turn, an individual's phenotype is affected by both biologically or nature-related factors, and knowledge and skill development and other experience-related "nurture" factors. Although we often see the phrase "nature versus nurture," human performance is a function of both. For example, in calculating the area of a rectangle, which is more important: length or width? This is a rather silly question because both are needed to calculate area and, thus, are of equal value. The same holds true for nature and nurture—both are required.

A particular *phenotype* defines an organism's observable trait characteristics, including such things as morphology (e.g., body height and mass), biochemical and physiological properties, and natural and learned behaviors. An individual human's phenotype results from the expression of that person's genetic makeup, as well as the influence of various environmental factors, including knowledge and skill development and prior experiences, and the interactions between these two major genetic and environmental forces. Why you and I look and act differently is because we have differing phenotypes, which, in turn, is primarily a product of our unique biology and combined environmental experiences (including learning).

These interdependent gene (nature) and environmental (nurture) forces can be diagrammed to demonstrate their interactive effects, as illustrated in Figure 2.4. Note in Figure 2.4 how both forces affect a specific phenotype,

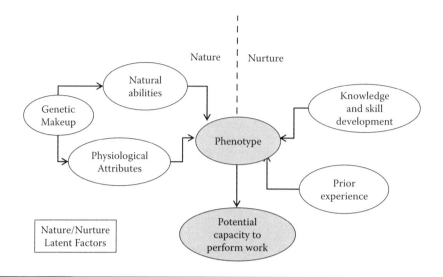

Figure 2.3 Expanded nature–nurture latent factors.

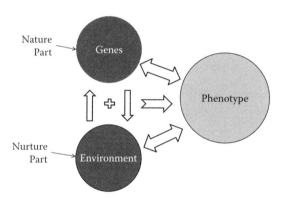

Figure 2.4 Interactive forces of genes and environment on phenotype.

as well as each other. Increasingly, scientists are discovering that our genes or genetic makeup affects our environment, and our environment affects our genes.

People often use the terms *ability* and *skill* interchangeably, implying that we can develop both via training. Yet, the two terms, especially to scientists who study human performance, have decidedly different meanings. *Abilities* represent stable and enduring traits that, for the most part, are determined by a person's individual genetic makeup or genotype. Such individual abilities include multilimb coordination, manual dexterity, arm–hand steadiness, dynamic strength, and gross body coordination, to name just a few.

Importantly, natural abilities *underlie* skilled performance and represent the "nature" part of the nature–nurture equation. Natural abilities, in some instances, also can limit potential performance levels by establishing genetically predetermined performance thresholds. As Roger Bannister, the first person to run a sub four-minute mile, was once quoted as saying, "Not all athletes are created equally."

Bannister's remark, although perhaps a bit insensitive in today's more politically correct world, never-the-less makes an important observation. Ability is primarily genetically or biologically determined and, in some instances, can limit the achievement of certain performance levels for certain individuals. For example, even in my much younger, more physically fit days, I could never have run a sub four-minute mile, no matter how hard I might have trained. I simply did not have the requisite genetic ability for such an extreme performance level. By comparison, I had a friend who could routinely run an almost sub four-minute mile (his best time was four minutes and seven seconds in a college-level track competition). Although my friend and I would sometimes run together, it was obvious that we were not "equally created" runners.

By comparison, producing a desired performance result as a function of practice (and in many instances, specialized training) represents a "nurtured" skill. Schmidt and Wrisberg (2004) define a *skill* as the capability of producing a desired performance result with maximum certainty, minimum energy or time, and developed as a result of practice. For the most part then, we are born with abilities, but must develop skills, often through training and practice.

Our genetic makeup governs our naturally determined abilities, as well as many physiological attributes, including a person's height and hair color. A *genotype* represents the genetic makeup of an organism. A genotype constitutes a unique and individual genetic code. As described by Tattersall (2012), an adult's anatomy is the end point of a developmental process that is heavily influenced, "… not just by the underlying genes themselves, but also by the sequence in which the genes are switched on and off; by exactly when this switching happens; and by how strongly the genes themselves are expressed while they are active."

Amazingly, 99.9 percent of a human's genes are the same as everyone else's. The observed genetic differences between two individuals are in the remaining 0.1 percent. This miniscule figure represents only one different nucleotide base in every 1,000. Yet that 0.1 percent or one in a thousand different nucleotide bases is still extremely important. It gives me blue eyes and a decidedly receding and graying hairline, while it may give you brown eyes and lots of thick red hair to comb.

As scientists began to decode and better understand the human genome (representing the complete set of genes that make us humans human), one futuristic hope was that they would discover a specific or individual gene associated with a particular ability, especially specific sports abilities. Having established this sought-after direct linkage between a specific gene and a particular ability, one could then potentially enhance an aspiring athlete's performance via some form of genetic engineering. Unfortunately, it now appears that a great number of genes are involved in determining a certain athletic ability, each one contributing only a small performance-related effect. However, when combined in some unique manner, those individual minor effects can result in a very large overall effect. Consequently, the potential for some type of single-gene human enhancement appears more science fiction than science nonfiction.

Wilhelm Johannsen, a Danish botanist, plant physiologist, and geneticist, in 1911 was one of the first people to draw a clear distinction between an organism's heredity (a genotype) and what that heredity produces (a unique phenotype). Johannsen understood that both genotype and environment are critical in developing a specific phenotype and expressed this observation in the following equation:

Genotype (G) + environment (E) + genotype and environmental interactions (GE) > phenotype (P)

Johannsen's genetic-environment formula is essentially the same formula graphically depicted in Figure 2.4.

Adrian Bejan, a J. A. Jones Distinguished Professor of Mechanical Engineering at Duke University, points out, however, that "nature, being born a certain way-it's a prerequisite for nurture." Consider, for example, swimming sensation and 22 Olympic medal winner Michael Phelps. One could certainly argue that Phelps was "biologically born" to swim.

Phelps stands 6'4" in height, yet supposedly has only a 32-inch inseam (about the same inseam measurement that someone who is 5'9" or 5'10" tall would normally have). He also has extremely long arms, massive and powerful shoulder muscles, and extra-large hands and feet. As described by Epstein (2013), Phelps' longer body trunk and shorter legs make for a greater surface area being in contact with the water when he swims. Epstein goes on to explain that this greater water surface contact area is akin to having a longer hull on a canoe. A "longer hull" creates a distinct advantage for moving through water at higher speeds.

Admittedly Phelps has spent countless hours in the pool practicing and mastering various swimming strokes, all under the watchful eyes of an expert coach. Yet, even given his admittedly superior nurture-centric training regime, one can still not deny his genetic or biological contribution—his longer hull—to his amazing swimming success story.

Such potential genetic contributions to performance are most evident in the thoroughbred horse racing world. My wife and I once toured a number of thoroughbred horse breeding farms just outside of Lexington, Kentucky. We were introduced to a number of top breeding stallions and learned how to "properly" introduce a thoroughbred horse. The breeders never just said this is "Joe, the racehorse." Instead, it was always this is "Joe, the racehorse" *and* his father was "Sam, the racehorse" *and* his mother was "Sally, whose father was the great racehorse, Jack." In thoroughbred horse racing, as my wife and I discovered, genetics matters.

However, as we all know, genetics can sometimes have a downside. For example, some might argue that, through intense inbreeding, Dalmatian dogs represent a genetics story gone astray. Although the black-spotted dogs might look cute on fire trucks and are adorable and lovable house pets, they often suffer from genetic defects, especially regarding their hearing. Reportedly:

■ 30 percent are born with some form of hearing defect.
■ 22 percent are born deaf in one ear.
■ 8 percent are born deaf in both ears.
■ In blue-eyed Dalmatians, 51 percent are born deaf in at least one ear.

As illustrated by this dog-related example, not all genetically induced phenotypes are success stories, especially when a species, or, in this case, a breed, is improperly bred.

Returning to our nature/nurture depiction as illustrated previously in Figure 2.3, a particular phenotype results in an individual's potential capacity to perform a specific task. As diagrammed in the figure, this phenotype-based potential capacity is a function of the individual's genetic makeup or biologically controlled genotype, and knowledge and skill development, enhanced by experience and repetitive practice. One of the main reasons why we often observe marked differences in performance levels by differing individuals performing the exact same task is because of wide differences in human genetic makeup and/or developed skill levels, that is, marked differences in one individual's phenotype in comparison to another individual's phenotype.

This nature–nurture continuum also affects intelligence or IQ. *Intelligence* represents a mental quality consisting of the ability to learn from experience, solve problems, and use knowledge to adapt to new situations. Intelligence is a function of both nature and nurture.

Originally, intelligence was defined as the ratio of mental age to chronological age times 100. On contemporary intelligence tests, average intelligence for a given age was a score of 100. This numerical figure meant that if you scored 100 on a standardized intelligence test, then you were considered to be of average intelligence. A score greater than 100 meant that you were "more intelligent" than the average person and were often described as having above-average intelligence. However, a score of less than 100 supposedly indicated that you were "less intelligent" than the average person.

The spread or distribution of these various standardized intelligence scores formed a nearly perfect symmetrical bell-shaped curve, also termed a normal curve. In a normal curve, most scores fall near the average (100), with fewer and fewer scores lying near the extreme ends (called the "tails" of the curve). In point of fact, in a normally distributed intelligence curve, 68 percent of all people score within 15 points above or below 100 (85–115). Additionally, 95 percent of all people fall within 30 points of that 100 average score (70–130). Thus, an intelligence score of greater than 130 implies a really smart person.

However, much has changed in our concept of intelligence since those earlier, standardized testing days. Today, there are numerous theories and associated tests regarding intelligence as summarized by Myers (2010). Some of these differing theories include:

■ *Spearman's general intelligence factor (g)*: A basic intelligence test that attempts to predict our abilities in varied academic areas. The theory suggests that different abilities, such as verbal and spatial abilities, do have some tendency to correlate.

■ *Thurstone's primary mental abilities*: Suggests that intelligence may be broken down into seven primary mental abilities: word fluency, verbal comprehension, spatial ability, perceptual speed, numerical ability, inductive reasoning, and memory. According to this theory, a single Spearman *g* score of intelligence is not as informative as individual scores for each of the identified seven primary mental ability areas.

■ *Gardner's multiple intelligences*: States that our abilities are best classified into eight independent intelligences, which include a broad range of skills beyond traditional "school smarts." According to this theory, intelligence is more than just verbal and mathematical skills. Other abilities are equally important to human adaptability.

■ *Sternberg's intelligence triarchic*: Intelligence is best classified into three areas that predict practical real-world success: analytical, creative, and practical. Additionally, these three facets of intelligence can be reliably measured.

Given the ongoing confusion and disagreement regarding the whole field of intelligence, from a work-centric, human performance perspective, the concept of *capability* may be more germane than that of intelligence. As defined by Schmidt and Wrisberg (2004), a capability represents characteristics of people that are subject to change as a result of practice and that represent a person's potential to excel in the performance of a task. Capability captures the essence of one's "potential capacity to perform work" and is a function of both ability and knowledge and skill development, and related experience and practice.

There also has been a great deal written about so-called emotional intelligence, especially in the pop-psychology literature. *Emotional intelligence* represents the ability to perceive, understand, manage, and use emotions. According to some researchers, emotional intelligence and IQ are not necessarily related.

Although the exact role of emotion in human performance is not fully understood, it should not be overlooked. Although, in many instances, genetic makeup and training may set the biophysical limits of human performance, personality traits often determine actual realized levels of performance.

Vassilis Klissouras (2001) offers strong support for the importance of this personality trait observation. In a published article, he describes two identical twin brothers who both competed in the same Olympic 20-km competitive walking event. One brother won the gold medal, whereas the other brother finished well back in the pack. Of special interest here is the fact that both brothers had undergone the exact same strenuous training regime under the same coach for the past 19 years prior to competing in the Olympics.

Additionally, biophysical testing of the identical twins revealed only minor and insignificant differences in physiological capacity. For example, percentage differences between the two brothers in body mass index, cardiac mass index, and percentage VO$_2$ max were all less than 5 percent. For all practical purposes, the two brothers had almost the exact same *physical* phenotype, as well as the exact same training, coaching, and race experiences.

Yet the twins tested very differently in measured personality traits. Percent difference in anger control was some 30 percent. Differences in reaction to anger were even more pronounced, measuring in the high 90 percent range.

Klissouras summarized his findings by noting that although possessing the right genetics and undergoing years of training are prerequisites for developing an Olympic athlete, ultimate success may be largely influenced by individual personality traits. This same observation may hold true in the non-Olympic workplace as well.

One of the real challenges in this entire nature–nurture discussion is in determining how to accurately assess an individual's "potential capacity to perform work." This topic has particular real-world relevance to the whole areas of personnel selection and talent management.

To better assess "potential performance capacity," many companies administer preemployment nature- and nurture-type tests (although they normally call them something else). For example, one high-tech company that I talked to on this subject was quite proud of its extensive test batteries that were routinely administered to potential employee candidates. However, when I asked them how derived test scores actually correlated with subsequent on-the-job performance, I received a blank stare and a rather embarrassed silence. My impression was that the company had never really thought about how their proctored tests actually predicted on-the-job performance; an unfortunate situation.

Although I am personally a fan of preemployment knowledge, skill, and ability testing, I am only a fan as long as some type of correlation between administered tests and subsequent on-the-job performance has been shown. For example, in basketball, some NBA teams have found that assessing a college player in the following three categories—2-point shooting efficiency, rebounds, and steals—provides a fair indication of how well that player will eventually perform at the professional level; in other words, those categories provide some indication of an individual's potential capacity to play basketball in the NBA. Like the NBA, private companies need to better ensure that their preemployment testing programs provide a similar, "fair indication" of subsequent on-the-job performance.

In summary, human performance, especially an individual's potential capacity to perform in the workplace, is primarily a function of a genetically *and* skill-influenced phenotype. Both nature- and nurture-related factors are prerequisites for human performance, with nature (ability) underlying nurture (skill).

I have personally evolved a great deal in my own thinking about the roles that nature and nurture play in human performance. When I first started my career in human performance, for example, I thought that almost any human performance-related problem could be solved by training (meaning that I was essentially a "nurture" kind of guy). As such, I spent much of my early career developing, delivering, and managing diverse training initiatives. If someone had a human performance problem, then send them to a training course.

Although I still greatly value the importance of well-developed and delivered training (and all other skill development activities for that matter), I now realize that training in the workplace is only one part of the human performance improvement equation. An equally important part is someone's innate ability or what the trainee brings to the classroom and, ultimately, to the workplace itself. In some instances, no amount of training, however well designed and delivered, can make up for a lack of innate ability. Such differences in innate ability essentially explain what happened in the two Tactical Response Force training courses described at the beginning of this chapter, or why some students passed the course, while others failed it.

Although an individual's potential performance capacity is heavily influenced by stable, genetically determined abilities and nurtured skill development, it is also influenced and modified by the immediate task setting and associated temporary conditions that humans sometimes experience in the workplace. This immediate workplace or task setting subject is described next.

Immediate Task Setting

When people *go* to work, they literally take with them a certain potential capacity to perform that work. However, once *in* a work setting, they now have an actual opportunity to physically perform the work. Performing that work is not only affected by their potential capacity (or what they bring with them), but also by the immediate task setting or the environmental work context itself.

As diagrammed in Figure 2.5, temporary human conditions (like having a really bad hair day), task demands, and other task-related environmental factors can sometimes interact in a manner to either positively or negatively

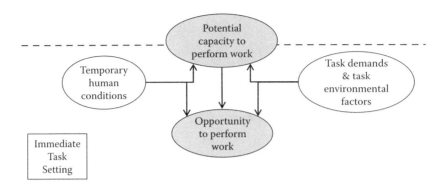

Figure 2.5 Expanded immediate task setting-related factors.

affect actual task performance. In some instances, task demands, especially under adverse or emergency-type conditions, can influence temporary human conditions, such as by increasing stress levels, which, in turn, can adversely affect human task performance.

Temporary human conditions may include fatigue, mood and motivational state, stress levels, and state of health. Fatigue, motivation, and stress levels can sometimes be influenced—either positively or negatively—by the task setting. Remember, for example, how Frank Gilbreth worked hard to lessen the fatigue level of his bricklayers by eliminating wasted motions and steps associated with the laying of each brick, rearranging the placement of the bricks and mortar to a more accessible and easily reachable location, and redesigning the scaffolding from which his bricklayers worked.

But how, for example, can a work setting affect motivation, defined as an internal need or drive that energizes and directs behavior, thus translating human potential into human action? In almost any work-related setting, one can be more or less "motivated" to perform a given task or perform that task in a given (and, hopefully, correct) manner.

One way to think about motivation is via a "formula" developed by Kurt Lewin (1890–1947). Lewin is a well-regarded pioneer in the fields of social, organizational, and experimental psychology. He is perhaps best known for his work in the area of force field analysis. However, his work in motivation is of equal importance, especially for our discussion here. According to Lewin, motivation, represented by what he termed intent, is equal to need times valence, divided by psychological distance, or

$$\text{Intent} = \text{Need} \times \text{Valence/Psychological Distance}$$

Lewin defines the various components in his motivation formula as follows:

■ *Intent* represents a psychological force to perform an act.
■ *Need* is a desire for some end state.
■ *Valence* represents the reward value of the end state.
■ *Psychological distance* represents all of the difficulties involved in performing a task or adopting the means necessary to reach a desired end state. I always like to think of psychological distance as the "hassle factor" associated with doing something.

I once heard a fascinating description of a psychology experiment that demonstrates quite vividly the importance of psychological distance. A group of Psychology 101 college students (the modern equivalent of white rats used in many earlier psychology experiments) were asked to follow a set of instructions involving mixing numerous glass beakers filled with different colors of water in an exact and precise manner. However, interspersed throughout the written water-mixing instructions were directions to don various types of safety equipment, such as rubber gloves, hair covering, and face shield.

Unbeknownst to the students, the real purpose of the experiment was to see how well they followed these safety equipment-related instructions. There were three different versions or conditions of the experiment. In one condition, all safety equipment was neatly laid out in an organized manner immediately next to the water-filled beakers. In the second experimental condition, the safety equipment was placed at a farther distance in the back of the room in a disorganized heap, requiring students to sort through the mangled array to find an individual piece of equipment. In the final condition, students had to leave the room, walk down a hallway, and search through a hallway cabinet where the safety equipment was intermixed with other laboratory supplies.

In this experiment, the concept of psychological distance was literally translated into physical distance and increasing disorganization, all representing an increasing "hassle factor." The results of the experiment are fairly intuitive. In the first experimental version with ready access to the safety equipment, all students donned the required equipment at the appropriate times and in the correct order. In the second version, a number of the students failed to don all of the equipment at the appropriate time. In the final version, students quickly lost interest (or motivation) to walk out of the room and search for the required safety gear in the hallway cabinet.

I think the described experiment points out a critical point: we can retool and redesign a work setting in such a way that we can influence the way in which people are *motivated* to perform tasks. Or, to put it another way, with careful thought, we can decrease the amount of psychological distance in any work setting, thus helping workers to perform tasks in a more correct manner.

The concepts of arousal and stress also can sometimes be an important determinant in human performance. As defined by Schmidt and Wrisberg (2004), *arousal* represents the level of action of the central nervous system. Arousal can vary from extremely low levels during sleep (or in extremely boring jobs) to exceptionally high levels during intense physical activity and excitement. A key concept of arousal is found in what is termed the inverted-U principle as graphically illustrated in Figure 2.6.

The *inverted-U principle* describes the relatively stable relationship between arousal level and performance. Normally, as a person's arousal level increases, his or her performance levels increase, but only up to a certain point. If a person's arousal level increases beyond that critical point (such as due to a high state of stress), then performance levels begin to decrease, as illustrated in Figure 2.6.

As further illustrated in Figure 2.7, arousal is often task-specific. For example, tasks that require fine motor skills and are cognitively complex, such as playing the piano, require lower states of arousal in order to achieve a maximum level of performance. By comparison, gross motor movements involving simple cognitive tasks, such as weightlifting, are best performed at high levels of arousal. Playing basketball, as illustrated in Figure 2.7, is situated somewhere in between these two arousal extremes. As such, there is a *zone of optimal functioning* for any given task (defined as the range of arousal levels associated with a person's maximum performance levels).

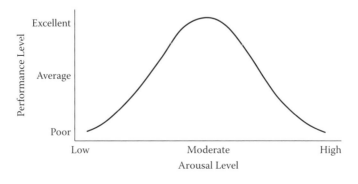

Figure 2.6   Generic inverted-U principle arousal curve.

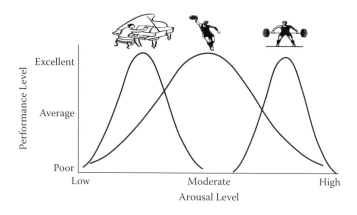

Figure 2.7   Task-specific arousal curves.

Very high levels of arousal result in an increase in adrenal hormones and associated blood supply to the extremities. Although increases in hormonal level and blood supply negatively affect fine motor skill performance, they often positively affect gross motor skill performance. Accordingly, if you are about to enter an archery competition, you probably want to try and chill out, and listen to more mellow, soothing types of music. However, if you are about to attempt to pump some serious iron, go with loud, "Born in the USA," upbeat-type music.

Stress, especially high levels of stress, represents arousal gone too far. Stress is usually a function of time and consequence; shorter times and greater consequences normally translate into greater levels of stress. Very high levels of stress can induce tunnel vision or perceptual narrowing. *Perceptual narrowing* is the narrowing of attentional focus that occurs as a person's arousal level increases.

The problem with perceptual narrowing is that sometimes a person can focus too much on one aspect of a problem, while overlooking other, equally critical aspects of the problem altogether. This overly narrow-focused situation can be especially dangerous in a medical emergency room setting or during an in-flight emergency. In fact, some pilots have become so engrossed in solving a flight-related emergency that they have forgotten to continue to monitor the plane's fuel level during the emergency. As a result of this neglected oversight, the plane literally ran out of gas before it could land or the onboard emergency could be successfully resolved.

I once met a supervisor who oversaw operations in a nuclear power plant control room that had a novel way of dealing with perceptual narrowing. He freely admitted that whenever there was a plant upset or emergency, he became entirely engrossed in trying to solve that problem. But, *before* he began to tackle the immediate problem, he always assigned someone to continuously monitor the overall operational state of the plant. In this way, he said that, although he had the "narrow eyes" on the immediate problem, someone always had the "wide eyes" on overall plant status and safety. This same "narrow- and wide-eyed" strategy can be adopted in other work settings as well.

One way to think about the immediate task setting, especially associated task demands and related task environmental factors (including needed work tools and other technologies), is that it literally provides the physical and social "context" in which humans work. Although a hospital emergency room and an aircraft-maintenance depot represent two very different work settings, they share one important trait in common—both settings provide work context.

In a well-designed work setting, that context can positively influence human performance. In a poorly designed setting, however, work context can negatively affect human performance. As such, context matters. That is why the disciplines of ergonomics and human factors are so important. Via more intelligent work and tool design, the two disciplines attempt to provide better context, creating a more productive, reliable, and safer work environment.

As will be described in much greater detail in Chapter 4, in some instances, a poorly designed work setting (a.k.a., a bad context) can set humans up to fail. Imagine, for example, that you work as a Central Alarm Station (CAS) operator. Your job is to monitor a bank of security-related video displays and alarms. If you see something suspicious on a video display or if an auditory alarm sounds, then you must communicate some type of response command to patrolling security personnel.

Now also imagine that day in and day out those security alarms go off on an almost daily, if not more frequent, basis. Wind, rain, scampering rodents, and just about everything else seems to trigger them. You have been on the job for some five years now and have dealt with literally hundreds if not thousands of false alarms, but *never* a real one. So, whenever an alarm sounds, you just "know" that it is a false one. Although, when an alarm does sound, you promptly radio security personnel per procedure to investigate the sounding alarm's location, you rarely have them respond in an urgent, lights-flashing, and speedy manner.

Then it happens. One day the alarm is real. However, you automatically assume it is false. That is how you have been conditioned to think about alarms over the years. Thus, by failing to respond in a rapid, lights-flashing, and driving fast manner, a major security incident takes place.

This fictional account is, unfortunately, all too real in some instances. As illustrated, a poorly designed work setting or, in this case, a poorly "alarmed" one, can often induce so-called human failure. Accordingly, just as humans can positively or negatively affect a work setting, so can a work setting positively or negatively affect those very same people. It really is a two-way street.

Note, as one descends each successive layer of my depicted model, the complexity of the model increases. This increasing complexity is primarily caused by the greater interactivity between and among the various elements comprising the individually defined, but overlapping model layers. As such, failed human performance may not be caused as much by any single, individual factor as graphically depicted in the model, but rather by some combination of factors that interact in an unwanted and often unanticipated manner.

Performance Outcome

The final layer in the developed model is the actual or realized performance level achieved during performing a given task. As illustrated in Figure 2.8, a derived task performance level can be either acceptable or not. Unfortunately, determining levels of "acceptability" without any predefined and in-place performance measurement system can prove difficult. It is interesting to observe how many organizations strive to quantitatively measure just about everything in their respective organization except human performance outcomes. Instead, they rely on antiquated and highly subjective, often behavior-based annual performance reviews to assess the performance levels of their employees. The value of quantitatively measuring human performance is that such developed measures cannot only assist in objectively determining if required levels of acceptability are successfully

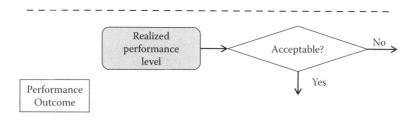

Figure 2.8　Performance outcome layer.

being achieved, but, if they are not, then the same measures also can be used for diagnostic purposes, helping to answer the "why not" question (see Harbour, 2009b; 2013b).

If a given performance level is unacceptable, then the next step is to determine why. Based only on the developed model presented here (much more is to come in subsequent chapters), any attempt to analyze and improve human performance must, as an initial starting point, focus on at least four major areas.

1. *Task analysis.* The first question that should always be asked in analyzing human performance is: Do we actually understand what humans must do to successfully perform a given task and how they must do it, and what tools and other resources are required, as well as what conditions or specifications of performance must be met? Answering this extended first question set usually starts with performing some type of task analysis (the "how" of which is described in much greater detail in Chapter 5). By understanding the basic elements of a task, the associated demands of the task (including possible imposed time constraints), and the immediate and surrounding task environment, we are in a much better position to more accurately and explicitly define the required human abilities and skills necessary to successfully perform the task. Unfortunately, in many instances, such analyses do not exist and instead, when something does go wrong, our immediate focus is on the supposed "failure" of the human involved in performing the task.

2. *Task design.* One of the easiest ways to improve human performance is to not directly focus on the human per se, but rather to first concentrate on attempting to redesign the task, the task demands, and/or the immediate task environment (e.g., work context). Of particular importance here is to always try and lessen the demands of the task whenever possible. For example, a recall cognitive task is much more mentally demanding than a simpler recognition task, especially a recognition task supported by a well-constructed job aid, such as a checklist. Supplying appropriate job aids that positively augment human performance and, thereby, lessen the mental demands of a task, is one very effective means of improving human performance and by association, overall task performance. The same concept goes for designing better displays, controls, and the tools that humans use to perform a given task. In this sense and as mentioned earlier, the disciplines of human factors and

ergonomics have a great deal to offer in improving human performance via their ability to more effectively design the task environment and the various tools used in that environment.

3. *Personnel selection.* Based on our derived understanding of the task, the task demands, its current or revised design, and the requisite human abilities and skills necessary to successfully perform the task, we must next ask if we have selected the right individual(s) to perform the task. It is always essential to determine if an individual has (or *had* in the case of an adverse incident investigation) the requisite natural abilities and skills necessary for successful task performance. Although it is important to recognize and respect individual differences, it also is necessary, in some instances, to realize that not everyone can successfully perform a given task due to a lack of innate natural abilities or developed skills and related practice. Such human realities should not be viewed as unfair discrimination, but rather simply as the very real-world need to select individuals who have the greatest probability for successful task performance.

4. *Training and development.* If a person possesses the natural abilities to successfully perform a task, he or she may still lack the corresponding necessary skills and requisite practice for successful task execution. In this case, additional training and practice can be of great benefit in improving task performance. However, it is of absolute importance to never view training as some magical panacea, as many organizations do. Admittedly, training and associated practice can represent very powerful interventions, but only if the problem is, in fact, a training- and practice-related problem. Unfortunately, if someone lacks the requisite natural abilities to perform a task, then normally no amount of training will bridge the gap between task success and task failure. Additionally, many skills are perishable and require a certain level of maintenance and continuing practice. Fulfilling this ongoing critical skill maintenance requirement in order to sustain effective human performance is often just as important as initially developing new work skills in the first place.

In summary, successful human task performance is dependent on a number of highly interdependent and interactive system elements, as illustrated in my developed macro model of human performance, now aggregated into a single model that is depicted in Figure 2.9. As graphically illustrated in the model, human performance is not only affected by a genetically and skill-influenced phenotype, but also by varying

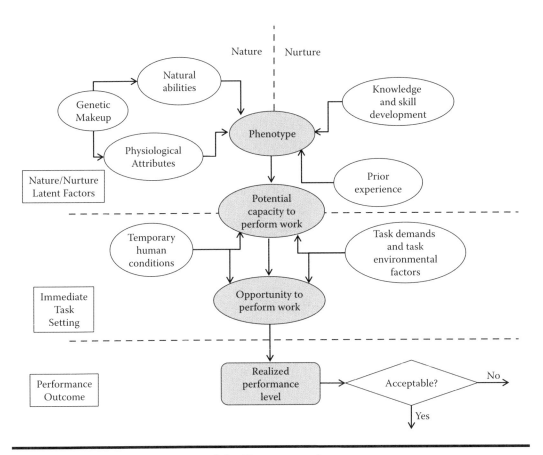

Figure 2.9 Combined macro model of human performance.

characteristics of the immediate task environment itself, all of which interact in a highly complex manner. Any attempt to improve human performance, therefore, must take into account all of these often competing and interacting variables. In many instances, failed human performance is actually more a function of a poorly designed and vulnerable work system than a supposedly fallible human. As such, it is important to consider *all* factors that may positively or negatively affect human performance in the workplace.

Chapter 3

A Micro Model: Perception, Cognition, and Action

In Chapter 2, a macro model of human performance was presented. In the constructed model, I noted that successful task performance is dependent on a number of highly varied system elements. As described in the chapter, performance is not only affected by a genetically and skill-influenced human phenotype (representing an organism's observable trait characteristics), but also by varying features of the immediate task environment, all of which interact in a highly complex and interdependent manner. One key finding of Chapter 2 is that initial personnel selection is often a critical "predeterminer" of subsequent human performance (including the actual trainability of an individual). Additionally, failed human performance is sometimes more a function of a poorly designed and vulnerable work system than a supposedly fallible human being.

One can also view human task performance from a microsystem perspective. At the individual task level and irrespective of task type or setting, human performance involves varying degrees of perception, cognition, and action. This *Perception–Cognition–Action* cycle, as illustrated in Figure 3.1, forms the basic building blocks of human performance at the immediate task level. In turn, failed human performance, including human error, often involves some failure of perception, cognition, and/or action.

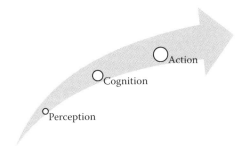

Figure 3.1   Perception–cognition–action (PCA) cycle.

By way of introduction to the perception–cognition–action cycle, perform the following four tasks in succession:

1. Raise your right hand.
2.
3. @#%! $*(^% #!~%$ ^&**%$* + = (%^#@
4. Complete 742 one-arm pushups within 30 seconds.

So, how did you do? I am sure almost everyone successfully completed Task #1 by correctly raising their right hand. For task #2, however, you probably thought that I left something out because you did not "see" anything printed. Without seeing something, you did not know what to do. Although you did see something printed for Task #3, it made absolutely no sense. Was this some type of major typographical error? And, finally, for Task #4, while you did see what was printed and most likely understood it, you also realized that it is not humanly possible to successfully perform the described task; no one can complete 742 one-arm pushups within 30 seconds.

As will be described in the following sections, each of these four tasks represents one or more components of the perception–cognition–action or PCA cycle.

The PCA Cycle

As introduced, the PCA cycle consists of perception, cognition, and action. *Perception* represents the process of detecting, organizing, and interpreting sensory information. It enables humans to recognize meaningful objects and events in their immediate environment. Perception results in a sensory input (called a *stimulus*) that is sent to the brain for further cognitive processing.

In Task #2, since nothing was printed, there was no sensory input or stimulus to send to the brain for subsequent processing. The PCA cycle was essentially stopped at the very beginning "P" part.

Cognition entails all of the mental processing activities associated with thinking: knowing and reasoning, remembering, and communicating. It involves various aspects of understanding, decision making, and action planning. Think of cognition as mostly brain stuff. In Task #3, although you could perceive a sensory input, it had no meaning; you could not understand it. Accordingly, without understanding, you were unable to make any decision or plan any task-related action as to what to do. In this failed task example, there was perception but no cognition.

Action involves the actual physical movement of the body, such as locomotion (powered by our legs) or the manipulation of an object (by using our hands). It represents a physical response to perception and cognition. Action is often the only physically observable part of the PCA cycle. That is, it is very hard to physically "see" someone sense a stimulus or mentally process that sensory input.

As humans, we have limitations or restrictions on what actions we can and cannot physically perform. In Task #4, for example, you quickly realized (through perception and cognition) that it is not humanly possible to perform the requested physical movement within the allotted 30-second timeframe. As such, knowing something about human physical limitations can allow us to better design work environments and more "human-doable" task sequences.

Sometimes in psychology textbooks, especially older ones, you see these hyphenated letters: *S-R.* "S" represents a stimulus or, in our case, perception. "R" is the response or action to that stimulus. The hyphen between the S and the R represents the cognitive processing that goes on between the presented stimulus and the physical response. Psychologists, especially cognitive psychologists whose primary focus is on studying how the brain processes information, often argue that all of the really interesting stuff is found "within the hyphen." Yet, from a human performance perspective, it is all important: the S, the R, and the hyphen. As such, our focus here is to better understand how perception, cognition, *and* action combine to lead to skilled performance.

Before continuing our discussion of the PCA cycle, however, it may prove helpful to first discuss the notion of "skill" in greater detail. An underlying concept of the PCA cycle is that successful task performance requires successful skilled performance.

Skill

As described in Chapter 2, a *skill* represents a capability; it is the capability of producing a desired performance result with maximum certainty, minimum energy or time, and developed as a result of practice (Schmidt and Wrisberg, 2004). Remember, whereas *ability* is a stable and enduring trait that for the most part is genetically determined, a skill is something that has to be acquired. Accordingly, we are not really born skilled, but simply abled. Finally, *capabilities* represent characteristics of people that are subject to change as a result of practice. They represent a person's potential to excel in the performance of a task.

As an example, finger dexterity is an ability that we are all born with. Keyboarding, however, is an acquired skill. Yet, keyboarding requires finger dexterity, which represents ability. A capable keyboarder is someone that can successfully perform the task of keyboarding via innate ability *and* developed skill. Ability thus underlies skill.

Skills are often classified as being either cognitive or motor. As defined by Schmidt and Wrisberg (2004), a *cognitive skill* is a skill for which the primary determinant of success is the quality of the performer's decisions regarding what to do. As such, a cognitive skill is a skill that emphasizes mainly knowing something, the "what to do." Playing chess primarily entails a cognitive skill.

A *motor skill* represents a skill for which the primary determinant of success is the quality (and often the speed) of the physical movement that the performer produces. Motor skills emphasize correctly performing the "what to do." A track and field athlete competing in the high jump is primarily a demonstration of a motor skill.

Motor skills can be further classified according to environmental predictability. A *closed skill* is a motor skill performed in an environment that is predictable or stationary. This type of task environment allows performers to plan their movements in advance (e.g., a gymnastics or high dive routine).

By comparison, an *open motor skill* is performed in an environment that is unpredictable or in motion. Open motor skills require performers to adapt their movements in response to dynamic properties of the environment. This type of unpredictability occurs in boxing, wrestling, and soccer, for example.

In a closed skill environment, the environment waits to be acted upon, allowing the performer to plan movements in advance. By comparison, in an open skill environment, the performer must use the processes of perception and decision making to adjust his physical movements, often in a short amount of time, in response to changing environmental conditions.

Additionally, Schmidt and Wrisberg note that motor skills can be classified by task organization. A *discrete skill* is a skill or task that is organized in such a way that the action is usually brief and has a well-defined beginning and end (e.g., catching, kicking, and throwing a ball, or firing a rifle). In turn, individual discrete skills can be aggregated into a serial skill.

A *serial skill* represents a type of skill organization that is characterized by several discrete actions linked together in sequence, often with the order of the actions being crucial to performance success (e.g., a gymnastics routine). For example, when shifting a manual transmission, it is critical to first depress the clutch prior to shifting gears. Performing the task in reverse order can result in a damaged transmission or clutch. Teaching a serial skill often involves first breaking the skill down into discrete individual parts, and then "recombining" those parts one discrete skill layer at a time, until the entire serial skill can be performed successfully.

Finally, a *continuous skill* is a skill organized in such a way that the action unfolds without a recognizable beginning or end in an ongoing and often unrecognizable manner. Swimming, running, and skating all represent continuous skills.

A skill also can be classified as a *perceptual-motor* or *psychomotor skill*. These skills involve both cognition and action. Psychomotor skills represent knowing what to do and being able to physically do it. For example, a ballet dancer must know what to do and in what order to do it in (the cognitive part of her dance routine). However, she also must possess the requisite motor skills to successfully perform an intricate ballet dance routine. Fortunately, with practice, many psychomotor skills become highly automated, merging cognition and action into a seamlessly executed "routine." Indeed when we watch a gifted ballet dancer perform, our focus is on the motor part of the psychomotor performance. We hardly even think about the cognitive part of the dance.

Often a more appropriate approach to classifying skill is to consider the degree to which perceptual and cognitive elements (i.e., knowing what to do) and motor elements (i.e., correctly physically performing that "what to do") contribute to successful skill performance. As depicted in Figure 3.2, a predominantly motor skill minimizes decision making, while maximizing motor control. A cognitive skill by comparison, such as playing chess, does just the opposite—maximizing decision making and minimizing

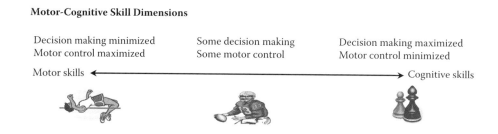

Figure 3.2 Motor-cognitive skill continuum.

motor control. A skill situated somewhat in the middle, such as driving an automobile or playing quarterback on a football team, involves both decision making and motor control.

Armed with this skill-related knowledge, a deeper understanding of the PCA cycle and its relationship to human task performance can be gained. To begin gaining this understanding, however, requires both a biological and a psychological understanding of human performance.

PCA Biology and Psychology

As described by Harbour (2013a) and graphically depicted in Figure 3.3, perception, cognition, and action involve sensing (resulting in perception), mental processing (resulting in cognition), and moving (resulting in action). This sensing, processing, and moving physiological *and* psychological model is wired together by our nervous system, which represents an integrated neural messaging or signaling subsystem. Although Figure 3.3 is depicted as a sequential circular model, it is important to point out that there are various feedback loops built into the model that are not shown.

Further, sensing, mental processing, physical movement, and neural signaling should not be thought of as separate or disconnected entities or microactivities. Rather, they are highly interconnected and interdependent. For example, most of us think that we only "see" with our eyes, but to actually see requires our eyes, our brain, and a connecting eye–brain optical nerve. Without first connecting our eyes to our brain via our optic nerve, we are unable to see.

Keeping this interconnected reality in mind, I will describe Figure 3.3 by each of its individual, but still interconnected and interdependent components.

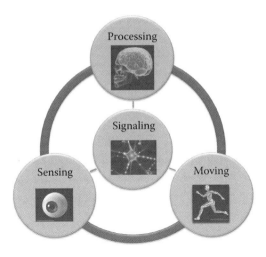

Figure 3.3 **Integrated sensing, processing, moving, and signaling model.**

Sensing

Sensing involves detecting an external stimulus or signal. It represents the beginning of the PCA cycle. Because humans perceive their environment (and reality) through their senses (via sight, hearing, taste, touch, and smell), sensing is how they actually get information into their minds to process. If something cannot be detected or sensed, then it cannot be transmitted to the brain for subsequent processing. Our senses, therefore, set limits on the kinds of data that we can and cannot process.

Every species seems to have a preferred or dominant sensory system. Starfish, jellyfish, and sea anemones primarily rely on touch. Bats, rabbits, and shrews mostly depend on detecting sound. Dogs, bears, and elephants rely to a great deal on smell. Apes, monkeys, and many birds are primarily vision-dominated.

Like monkeys and apes, a human's dominant sensory system is vision (although we also rely heavily on the senses of hearing and touch in the workplace). To indicate this visual sensory dominance, the human visual system uses a greater portion of the brain and more nerve cells to process and transmit visual information than any of the other senses. As such, human interpretation of a situation is often strongly biased toward what one can and cannot literally see.

Surgeons, for example, sometimes leave foreign objects in a patient during the final stages of an operation. This error of omission often leads to potentially severe postoperative complications. In this example, "out of sight" (or lack of visual sensing) is truly out of mind, much to the chagrin and pain of the affected patient.

To see, the human eye acts somewhat like a camera. The pupil first lets light in. Then the lens of the eye gathers and focuses this light, which is next registered as an image on the retina. Finally, the retina-registered image is transmitted to the brain via the optic nerve.

Our ability to see varies greatly from individual to individual. Some of us have normal and unaided 20/20 visual acuity. Others of us can only achieve this 20/20 visual acuity figure with the aid of glasses, contact lenses, or, in some instances, by way of surgery. But what does that 20/20 visual acuity figure actually mean?

If you are tested at a distance of 20 feet and can read the same line of letters that a person with normal vision can read at 20 feet, then your vision is 20/20. If the letters that you can just barely read correctly at 20 feet are large enough that a person with normal vision can read them at 40 feet, then your vision is 20/40.

Epstein (2013) describes the fascinating work of ophthalmologist Dr. Louis J. Rosenbaum regarding the almost extraordinary vision of most Major League Baseball players. Particularly impressive are day-to-day players or those players who play the infield or outfield, and bat on a regular basis. Rosenbaum found that such players average an amazing 20/11 visual acuity in their right eye and 20/12 vision in their left eye. Some players even tested out at 20/8, thought to be the theoretical limit of human vision. This almost supernatural visual acuity is certainly one reason why professional baseball players can hit a fastball pitch.

Many people are either nearsighted (myopia) or farsighted (hyperopia). In nearsightedness, light rays come to a focus too soon, which means that close objects can be seen clearly, but far objects are blurred. For farsighted people, just the opposite occurs. Light rays come to a focus too late. This light ray "lateness" causes distant objects to be seen clearly, but nearer objects to be blurred.

Partial color blindness is a visual problem in some humans, especially males. Color blindness is caused by a paucity or absence of different cone types in the eye: blue (which transmit short wavelengths of light), green (medium wavelengths of light), and/or orange (longer wavelengths of light).

We also do a great deal of sensing with our ears. Sound (or what we hear) is produced by traveling changes in air pressure that reach the ears. Our ability to detect sound depends upon the intensity or volume of the sound, and the frequency of the sound. Higher frequency sounds are said to be high pitched, whereas lower frequency sounds are described as low pitched. Just as the optic nerve serves to transmit visual images to the brain, sounds are transmitted to the brain via the auditory nerves. Indeed, all of our senses (including touch) are hard-wired to the brain.

As we get older, we often begin to lose the ability to hear high-pitched sounds, such as the chirping of a bird. With progressive hearing loss, we begin to lose the ability to hear lower frequency sounds as well.

Hearing often means that we must direct our ears to actively tune into selected sounds, while at the same time, tuning out unwanted sounds. A person who is unable to tune in some sounds and tune out other sounds is unable to follow a conversation in a noisy environment. This inability to discriminate among differing sounds is termed cocktail party syndrome or CPS. It is a very common problem, affecting at least 20 percent of the population. It also seems to affect both old and young people equally, as well as males and females.

In most work settings, smell is not a primary sensor. In newborn babies, however, smell is initially the most developed sense. This early development of smell is used to help babies locate their mother's breast milk. Also, "bad" smells, such as the smell of smoke, alert humans to possible danger. Additionally, we reportedly recall smells with 65 percent accuracy after a year, while the visual recall of photos declines to about 50 percent after only three months.

Most albino humans and animals have a defective ability to smell (termed partial anosmia). For many animals in the wild, partial anosmia reduces their chances of survival. This reduced survival rate may, in part, account for the relative rarity of albinism in nature.

To smell requires olfactory sensory receptors in the nose. Humans have about 5 million nose receptors. By comparison, dogs have some 125 to 300 million receptors in their noses. This huge number of olfactory receptors allows dogs to identify smells somewhere between 1,000 to 10,000 times better than humans. To process all these smell-related inputs, the proportion of a dog's brain that is devoted to analyzing smell is some 40 times greater than in humans. Whereas, for humans, seeing is believing; for dogs, smelling is definitely believing.

Like smell, taste is normally not a primary sensor in the workplace. Interestingly, we seem to remember good and bad tastes much longer than we do visual stimuli. Perhaps this is one reason why we often allow certain foods only a single taste test before deciding whether we do or do not like them. Additionally, our sense of taste is greatly influenced by our sense of smell. That is, something that does not smell good normally does not taste good, either.

As we age, the number of taste buds on our tongues begins to degrade. This is one reason why older people often use more and more pepper to get the same equivalent spice "sensation" as they received at a younger age with less. In stark contrast, the taste buds of very young children may be over-sensitive to some tastes, especially spicy foods.

Unlike smell and taste, touch is an important workplace sensor. For example, when we drive a vehicle, we primarily use our visual and touch sensory systems (along with hearing). In this driving example, we receive stimulus inputs from the "feel" of the steering wheel through our hands.

Although we can receive touch- or tactile-related inputs from essentially anywhere on our body, it is primarily what we feel with our hands (and sometimes our feet) that is often the most important. For example, humans very much use the sense of touch in the perception and manipulation of hand-held objects, particularly hand-held tools. In fact, as I now depress individual keys on my computer keyboard while writing this chapter, I receive a type of touch feedback (called *haptic* feedback) each time I tap a letter or numerical key. Unfortunately, this haptic-type feedback is missing on tablet computer and smartphone "glass" screens. This makes keyboarding on these types of devices difficult for some people. In order to provide sensory feedback in such instances, some tablet computer and smartphone manufacturers use sound as a haptic-feedback substitute.

Successfully using our various senses in the workplace to detect critical task-related signals is not always easy, however. For example, humans routinely suffer from what is termed *vigilance decrement*, which represents the deterioration in a person's ability to remain vigilant or alert for critical signals over time. Decrements in vigilance are indicated by a sharp decline in the rate of correctly detecting presented signals as a function of time. This sharp decline, in turn, is primarily a function of the number of signals presented. A generic vigilance decrement curve is illustrated in Figure 3.4.

A key contributor to vigilance decrement is human fatigue, often occurring over a surprisingly short period of time. To counteract the negative effects of vigilance decrement, many visual displays are automatically alarmed. In these instances, if a certain parameter strays outside of an established limit or threshold, an auditory alarm sounds. This display-alarming technique is especially important in improving the performance of critical human monitoring and system supervisory tasks. However, and as briefly discussed in the previous chapter, alarming a display may introduce the problem of false or spurious alarms.

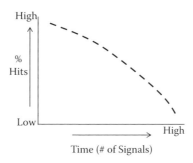

Figure 3.4   Generic vigilance decrement curve.

In some instances, it is impossible to alarm a visual display. For example, at airports, the x-ray display of our carry-on luggage undergoing routine security screening cannot be alarmed. Instead, it requires a security agent to visually observe the screen as each piece of luggage passes through the x-ray scanning machine. To counteract the effects of vigilance decrement in this particular instance, TSA (Transportation Security Administration) agents are constantly rotated in and out of this demanding monitoring task environment. This frequent in-and-out shuffling of security agents hopefully keeps a new, alert, and fresh set of eyes constantly on the screening process.

In summary, how we perceive our environment is through our senses. No detection means no subsequent processing. Accordingly, everything in the PCA cycle begins with the ability to detect some sensory input. Creating signal "noisy" or busy work environments that make individual signal detection difficult, or displaying signals with low signal strength and thus, low detectability, all add up to a work setting where critical sensory inputs may be unintentionally missed. Thus, in designing human-friendly work settings, always think about sensing and what signals must be detected and how they can best be detected. Additionally, as will be described in Chapter 8, many human errors are related to a lack of sensing.

As illustrated previously in Figure 3.3, any successfully sensed or detected signal is sent to the brain for mental processing—a topic that is explored next.

Processing

Processing involves understanding, deciding, action selection, and action planning, and is normally based on receiving a detected signal. Without initially sensing an information input, we cannot mentally process it.

Mental processing is mostly brain stuff. The human brain is a truly remarkable organ. Some interesting brain factoids include:

- Humans have the largest brain as a percentage of total body weight (~2 percent) of all organisms.
- The weight of an adult human brain is about 3 pounds, with some minor variation in size between males and females. At birth, the brain weighs approximately 0.8 pounds.
- The brain feels like a ripe avocado, is wrinkled like a walnut, and looks pink in color due to the blood flowing through it. It is also about the size of a cantaloupe.
- The brain is suspended in cerebrospinal fluid (CSF) within the skull. This fluid acts as both a cushion to protect the brain from physical impact and as a barrier to infection.
- The left side of the brain controls the right side of the body and vice versa.
- The brain consists of about 75 percent water. The brain is also the fattest organ in the body.
- The brain uses about 20 percent of the blood circulating in the body and 20 percent of the body's total oxygen supply. The human brain is thus a huge energy sink when it comes to blood and oxygen requirements. Without these two critical requirements, the brain can suffer potentially serious injury and even death in a matter of minutes.
- There are no pain receptors in the brain. Consequently when you have a headache, it is really not your brain that is hurting.
- Reportedly after the age of 30, the brain begins to shrink about 0.25 percent in mass each year. The good news is that through use, such as learning something new, we can add new nerve cells to the brain. So, like many other things pertaining to the human body, use it or lose it.

The fundamental building blocks of the brain and nervous system are individual nerve cells called *neurons*, which represent basic nerve cells. Neurons are composed of a cell body with dendrites or projections that bring information to the cell body, and axons that take information away from the cell body to another neuron, gland, or muscle.

A *synapse* is a small gap at the end of a neuron that allows information to pass from one neuron to the next. Synapses are found where nerve cells connect with other nerve cells, as well as where nerve cells connect with muscles and glands. The role of a synapse is to transmit (send and receive) electrochemical messages.

There is some indication that Alzheimer's disease occurs when neuron transmissions or synapses in the brain begin to become interrupted and blocked by plaque. This supposed plaque-caused blockage literally kills the brain one neuron at a time. Perhaps someday, plaque-eating, nano-sized robots will be used to routinely "clean out" our brains before damaging plaque can develop. Just as we now go to the dentist for an annual tooth-cleaning session, we may in the foreseeable future go to our favorite neurologist for an annual brain cleaning session. And because there are no pain receptors in the brain, that session should not hurt.

Scientists estimate that there are approximately 1,000 billion neurons in the human body, 100 billion of which are found in the brain alone (interestingly, the left hemisphere of the brain supposedly has about 186 million more neurons than the right hemisphere). During early pregnancy, neurons develop at the rate of 250,000 neurons per minute. This early and rapid neuron development is one reason why prenatal care is so important for developing babies. It is also why alcohol and drug use by mothers can be so detrimental to a developing fetus, as these stimulants can negatively affect normal neuron development in a young fetus.

There are two hemispheres to the brain: a right one and a left one. Each hemisphere controls movement in the opposite or contralateral side of the body. That is why a stroke affecting the right side of the brain affects the left side of the body. Additionally, each hemisphere of the brain can specialize in performing a specific and unique cognitive and perceptual function.

The two hemispheres of the brain are separated by a large bundle of fibers termed the *corpus callosum*. Although many people talk about being right- or left-brain dominated, in truth, it takes both hemispheres—the right *and* left hemisphere—to function and process information normally. As such, no one really wants to be right- or left-brain dominated.

Some key features of the brain include the cerebral cortex, the cerebellum, and the brain stem. The brain stem is the most primitive part of the brain. It consists of a group of structures that lie deep within the brain. The brain stem plays an important role in maintaining homeostasis or a stable state of equilibrium for controlling autonomic functions, such as breathing, heart rate, and blood pressure.

In turn, the cerebellum primarily monitors and regulates motor behavior, particularly automatic movements of the body. Although the cerebellum accounts for only about 10 percent of the brain's total weight, it contains more neurons than all of the rest of the brain combined.

Of most interest to the subject of human performance, however, is the outermost layer of the brain, which is termed the *cerebral cortex*. As described by Hawkins (2004), the cerebral cortex is the really intelligent part of the brain. Although only about one fourth of an inch thick and, when unfolded, about the size of a large cloth napkin, it contains some 10 billion tightly packed neurons.

The cerebral cortex is further divided into four major lobes: frontal, parietal, occipital, and temporal. Those four lobes represent the body's ultimate information processing centers. What makes you you and me me is greatly controlled by our own individual cerebral cortex, and all of the individual memories and experiences stored within it.

The frontal lobes (one in each hemisphere) are that portion of the cerebral cortex lying just behind the forehead. They are the largest of the brain's cerebral cortex structures, occupying some 41 percent of the cerebral cortex, and are the main site of higher cognitive functioning. The frontal lobes are primarily involved in speaking and muscle movements, and in making plans and judgments.

The parietal lobe (occupying 19 percent of the cerebral cortex) is that portion of the cerebral cortex lying at the top of the head and behind the frontal lobes. The role of the parietal lobe is to receive sensory input for touch and body position. This received input, in turn, builds a coherent picture of the world around us.

The occipital lobes (occupying 18 percent of the cerebral cortex) are that portion of the cerebral cortex lying at the back of the head. These lobes represent the primary visual area of the brain, receiving visual information from the eye's retina transmitted via the optic nerve. To see, therefore, requires not only our eyes and optic nerves, but also visual processing within the occipital lobes as well. In some instances, a very hard knock on the back of the head, such as caused by a nasty fall, may temporarily affect vision.

The temporal lobes (occupying 22 percent of the cerebral cortex) represent that portion of the cerebral cortex lying roughly above each ear. The temporal lobes contain a large number of substructures whose functions include perception, face and object recognition, memory acquisition, understanding of language, and emotional reactions. The parietal lobes also include the auditory areas. Each temporal lobe receives auditory information from the opposite ear. Thus, sound entering the right ear is actually processed on the left side of the brain.

An alternative and nonbiological way to view the role of the brain in the PCA cycle is to think of it as a very complex information processing unit, somewhat akin to how a computer processes information (however, this computer-related analogy should be taken only so far). In this information processing view, the brain takes in various sensory inputs and sends out action signals via the nervous system to the body's muscles. Although various information processing models have been developed, they all more-or-less share the same common characteristics as that depicted in Figure 3.5.

As illustrated in the figure, information from the environment (representing a sensory input) first enters what is termed *sensory memory,* which represents the immediate, very brief recording of sensory information in the memory system. Most of that information is immediately forgotten. However, some sensory inputs are transferred or encoded to our short-term memory. *Encoding* is simply the processing of information further into the memory system.

As in sensory memory, much of the information transferred to short-term memory is quickly forgotten. Also called *working memory,* our short-term memory represents "activated" memory that holds a few items briefly, such as a fleetingly memorized phone number while dialing, before the information is forgotten.

In 1956, Princeton University cognitive psychologist George A. Miller observed that individuals can normally retain or process only seven, give or take two, items of information in their correct serial order in their short-term or working memory. This observation is often referred to as Miller's Law of Seven (+/−2). It is one reason why phone numbers contain seven digits, zip codes five digits, and social security numbers nine digits.

One way to enhance the amount of information that we can retain in our short-term memory is through *chunking,* which involves organizing items into familiar and manageable units. It often occurs automatically. For example, our home phone numbers contain an area code, three prefix numbers, and four additional numbers, or (xxx) yyy-zzzz. However, we

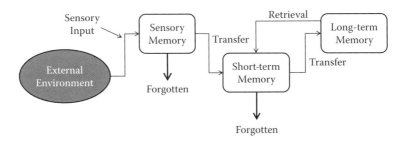

Figure 3.5　Simple information processing model.

normally memorize our home phone number not as 10 individual numbers, but as three "chunks" of numbers.

Read the following numbers, then immediately close your eyes and recite them in sequential order: 1492177619331949199420012014. Of the 28 numbers, how many did you correctly remember? You probably remembered some five to nine numbers. Yet, I can easily recall all 28 numbers each and every time. How can I do this? It is easy. The numbers represent a list of dates that have specific meaning to me: 1492–1776–1933–1949–1994–2001–2014. So, instead of remembering 28 numbers, I am actually only recalling seven different chunks or groupings of number, well within Miller's Law of Seven (+/–2). Therefore, if you want to expand your working memory, then chunk away.

In some instances, information is transferred from our short-term memory to our long-term memory for permanent storage (often as a result of rehearsal). *Long-term memory* represents the relatively permanent and limitless storehouse of the memory system. It stores all of our knowledge, skills, and experiences. It is this stored information that we retrieve. *Retrieval* is the process of "withdrawing" or getting information out of memory storage. In many instances, why we cannot remember something is not so much a problem of permanent storage, but rather a problem of retrieval.

Stored information often becomes highly automated through learning, repetition, and endless hours of rehearsal. For example, when we are driving our car and come to a red stoplight, we seem to automatically know what to do (stop) and how to do it (take foot off gas, put foot on brake); we do not really "think" about it. This automatically developed behavior is a result of learning and endless hours of practice behind the wheel. Author Mark Bowden (1999), in describing the incredible skills of military Special Operations helicopter pilots, captures this type of automated behavior perfectly when he notes that "… their moves in the electronic maze of their cockpits were so well rehearsed they had become instinctive."

Unfortunately, one reason why new drivers (especially young teenagers) are at times so dangerous behind the wheel is that some of their driving skills have yet to become fully automated. That is, driving has yet to become "instinctive." Consequently, young teenage drivers sometimes are still thinking about what to do when they should (urgently) be doing it.

In later chapters, specific ideas for improving human information processing capabilities are offered, such as the use of checklists and other cognitive aids. Additionally, many emerging "smart" technologies can greatly aid mental processing and some of the imposed limitations of human memory.

For example, in the past if I wanted to call John Smith, I would have to look up his phone number in the telephone book, commit it to my short-term memory, and then retain that number long enough to correctly dial him. Sometimes, however, I would forget Smith's number while dialing and would have to look it up again, necessitating bothersome rework.

Now with my Apple iPhone, all I have to do is look up John Smith under my "contacts" icon. Once I open John Smith's contact page, I simply press his entered number and the phone automatically dials it for me. This smartphone process no longer requires me to briefly hold John Smith's telephone number in my short-term memory. As long as I can still remember and retrieve the name of John Smith from my long-term memory, and I have previously entered his phone number correctly into my iPhone, I am good to call. In this example, my need to rely on short-term memory to complete a simple task has been essentially eliminated.

The final component of the PCA cycle is action, represented by physical movement. But before discussing this final component, now may be a good time to describe the "wiring" linking the PCA cycle together, here represented by neural signaling.

Neural Signaling

To successfully perform Task #1, which involved raising your right hand, required:

- A sensory input being sent from your eye to the brain via your optic nerve
- A "raise right hand" signal or message being sent from your brain down your spinal cord and out to the muscles in your right arm

These required signaling and messaging tasks are accomplished through the nervous system, an incredible wiring system that ties the whole PCA cycle together.

The *nervous system* represents the body's speedy, electrochemical communication or signaling network. It consists of all of the nerve cells of the central and peripheral nervous subsystems as summarized in Figure 3.6.

There are two primary types of nerve cells or neurons that comprise the nervous system: sensory neurons and motor neurons. *Sensory neurons* carry incoming information from the sensory receptors (i.e., eyes, ears, etc.) via the peripheral nervous system to the central nervous system. In turn, *motor neurons* carry outgoing messages from the brain and spinal cord

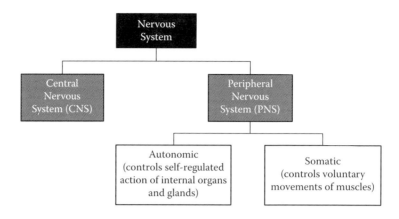

Figure 3.6 Nervous system structure.

(comprising the central nervous system) to muscles and glands via the peripheral nervous system. One can think of this sensory- and motor-neuron routing system as representing a somewhat "closed loop," with incoming sensory information going to the brain and outgoing action or motor messages coming from the brain.

The *central nervous system* or CNS includes the brain and spinal cord. In the CNS, signals are continuously being transmitted up and down the spinal cord, and to and from the brain. The basal portion of the brain stem continues directly into the cylindrical bundle of nerve fibers that make up the spinal cord. The spinal cord is encased in a protective sheath called the spinal dura mater that, in turn, is housed in a central "tunnel" within the various vertebrae comprising the spine or backbone. Each vertebra contains an opening called a vertebral canal. When individual vertebrae and vertebral canals are aligned, the spinal cord fits perfectly within the backbone.

As described by Powers and Howley (2007), some evidence suggests that the spinal cord itself (along with the brain) plays an important role in signaling voluntary muscle movement, with groups of neurons controlling certain aspects of motor activity. The concept of *spinal tuning* describes this spinal-related mechanism by which a voluntary movement signal is translated into appropriate muscle actions. Accordingly, a rather general "raise your right arm" signal may initially be sent from the brain, which is then broken down into more detailed instructions as that message travels through the spinal cord—something possibly like "muscle X you do this" and "muscle Y you do something different."

The *peripheral nervous system* or PNS is that portion of the nervous system located outside of the spinal cord and brain. The PNS is divided into the *autonomic nervous system* that controls self-regulated action of internal organs and glands (like the beating of the heart), and the *somatic nervous system.* The somatic nervous system controls voluntary movements of skeletal muscles, our primary interest here. Whereas the CNS appears fairly neat and tidy, the PNS looks something like a crazed maze of wires going every which way.

Various nerves of the PNS branch off from the spinal cord and, as noted, essentially go everywhere, from the tips of our fingers to the bottoms of our toes. It is these PNS-related nerves that signal pain to the brain when we stub a toe or smash a finger.

To accommodate this outward branching of peripheral nerves from the spinal cord, there is a space between adjacent vertebrae called intervertebral foramina. As peripheral nerves branch off the spinal cord, they exit through these foramina openings. Consequently, the spine (and all associated vertebrae) serves not only to support our bodies, allowing us to stand, bend, and twist, but it also functions as a very important protective conduit system for the central and peripheral nervous systems.

Thus, sensory signals are sent from the peripheral nervous system to the central nervous system for processing. In turn, voluntary muscle movement signals or messages are sent from the CNS out through the PNS to the involved muscle groups. Accordingly, the PNS plays an important role in not only linking our sensing subsystem to our brain-dominated processing subsystem (via the spinal cord), but also in connecting our action subsystem to our brain (once again via the spinal cord). Unfortunately, many spinal cord injuries prevent this critical transmission between the central and peripheral nervous systems. This is one reason why serious spinal cord injuries often lead to paralysis in the affected limbs—signals can no longer be transmitted to and from the CNS to the PNS.

In summary, our nervous or signaling system plays an important role in linking the perception–cognition–action cycle together. Without these critical linkages, sensory inputs cannot be transmitted to the brain, nor can voluntary movement messages be communicated from the brain to corresponding muscle groups. As noted, one critical role of the nervous system is to signal voluntary movement, a topic explored next.

Moving

Once a sensory input has been transmitted to the brain via the nervous system for processing, an action- or movement-oriented "do something" decision is often made. Accordingly, the final step in the PCA cycle is to physically execute that selected "do something" action. Such physical action almost always requires moving at least some part of the body.

There are two basic types of human movement: gross movement and fine movement. *Gross motor movement* emphasizes the control and coordination of large muscle groups in relatively forceful activities, such as in weightlifting and soccer. By contrast, *fine motor movement* involves the coordination and control of small muscle groups that must be tuned precisely. Fine motor movement also normally involves some aspect of eye–hand coordination, as in repairing a watch or performing surgery. As described earlier in Chapter 2, high states of arousal can often positively affect gross motor movement, whereas such high arousal states negatively interfere with fine motor movement.

Movement is actually quite complex and involves the interaction of the following:

- *Bones,*
- Linked together by *joints,*
- That are moved by the actions of *muscles,*
- Which, in turn, are fueled by oxygen-carrying *red blood cells.*

The human skeleton represents a mobile framework of bones, which provide rigid support for the body. Bones also serve as levers for the action of muscles that are critical for movement. There are some 206 bones in the adult human skeleton, although this number varies slightly between individuals and with age.

Some interesting bone factoids include:

- The longest bone in the human body is the thigh bone or femur. It is about one fourth of the height of a person. The smallest bone is the stirrup bone found in the ear. It measures approximately 1/10 of an inch.
- Humans and giraffes have the same number of vertebrae in their neck (7). In a giraffe, however, these seven cervical vertebrae are much larger and longer.
- Bone tissue consists of about two-thirds mineral components, mostly in the form of calcium salts, which provide rigidity. Approximately one third of a bone is comprised of organic components, which affords some elasticity. Without rigidity, bones would lose their shape. However, without elasticity, they would easily shatter.

- Bones are subjected to differing types of mechanical stresses, including:
  - Gravitational pressure from the body itself, especially experienced while standing.
  - Gravitational pressure from external objects, such as when someone carries a heavy suitcase.
  - Movement against resistance stresses, such as when we attempt to lift a heavy object and at first that object does not move.

Certainly one of the more interesting bones in the human body is the hyoid bone. The hyoid is a U- or horseshoe-shaped bone that protects the windpipe. It is located between the mandible (lower jawbone) and larynx, and beneath the base of the tongue. What makes the hyoid so unique is that it is the only bone in the human body that is *not* articulated or attached to any other bone. Rather, the hyoid bone is held in place by several muscles and a single ligament. As an occasional reader of courtroom legal fiction, the hyoid bone is sometimes mentioned in relation to a strangling-caused murder case. When someone is strangled, the hyoid bone is frequently fractured, an almost sure sign of foul play.

Joints represent areas where bones are linked or connected together. The various joints of the skeleton have varying degrees of mobility. However, without joints, there would be no skeletal movement.

Humans have over 230 moveable and semimoveable joints in their bodies. Differing types of skeletal joints are based on the shape of corresponding articulating surfaces. The shoulder and hip joint, for example, represent ball-and-socket joints. In a ball-and-socket joint, one surface is roughly spherical and the other is cup-shaped. This configuration allows movement in all directions. It is also the reason why the shoulder joint is one of the most flexible joints in the human body. Unfortunately, however, this high degree of shoulder flexibility sometimes comes at a painful price. The shoulder joint is one of the least stable of our skeletal joints, as it is set in a very shallow socket. This shallow joint configuration is one reason why a dislocated shoulder is such a common bone-related injury in many contact sports; it can easily be "disjointed."

Elbow and knee joints are called hinge joints. In a hinge joint, the convex surface of one bone fits against the concave surface of the other bone in a clasping-type arrangement. Movement in a hinge joint is primarily in one plane only, allowing for flexion and extension.

Our ability to rotate our neck is made possible by what is called a pivot joint. In a pivot joint, a pointed or rounded process of one bone fits securely into a ring-like structure of another bone. The two upper cervical vertebrae in our neck involving the atlas (the first cervical vertebra, designated as C1) and the axis or second cervical vertebra (C2) represent a pivot-type joint.

An especially important bone and joint success story is the human hand. Our hands represent very versatile tools capable of performing tasks ranging from fine precision (playing the piano or threading a needle) to great strength (swinging a sledgehammer or opening a stubborn jar lid). Indeed, our success as a species is due in large part to our ability to grasp and manipulate objects. As such, humans truly are the ultimate hand tool-using species.

A key aspect of the human hand is the opposable thumb. An opposable thumb makes grasping possible and is controlled by nine individual muscles, which, in turn, are controlled by three major hand nerves. Without the thumb, the human hand loses many of its remarkable functions.

Perhaps to indicate the importance of the human hand, approximately 25 percent of our brain's cerebral cortex's motor cortex is devoted solely to managing and coordinating the muscles in our hands. In total, a human hand contains some 29 bones, 29 joints, 123 ligaments, and 34 muscles.

Whereas bones function as levers, muscles serve as versatile motors to "move" those levers. The human body contains over 600 skeletal muscles, which constitute 40 to 50 percent of a human's total body weight. One of the largest muscles in the human body is the gluteus maximus muscle located in the buttocks. The smallest skeletal muscle is the stapedius muscle located deep within the inner ear.

Skeletal muscles (also known as voluntary or striated muscles) are attached to bones and when contracted, produce movement. In order to produce movement, one end of a muscle is attached to a bone that does not move (called the *origin*), while the opposite end is fixed to a bone that is moved during muscular contraction (called the *insertion*). For example, our tricep and bicep muscles allow us to bend and straighten our arm due to their dual "origin and insertion" attachments. Interestingly, the only muscle in the body that is not connected on both ends is the tongue, a surprisingly strong muscle.

Finally, muscles need fuel to function. That fuel is supplied by red blood cells that contain hemoglobin. Hemoglobin is used for the transport of oxygen via the circulatory system (veins and arteries), all pumped by the heart. Our arteries transport oxygenated blood from the left side of the heart to all regions of the body. One reason why some athletes, especially those in competitive cycling, attempt to "blood dope" or replace a portion of their own blood supply via illegal blood transfusions is to increase their blood's oxygen content or hematocrit. This increased oxygen content is critical for performing more efficiently (and less "fatiguing") in long-distanced endurance sports.

Putting it all together, movement requires bones, joints, muscles, oxygenated blood, and voluntary muscle messages that are sent through the peripheral nervous system. Although simply raising your right hand may seem rather trivial, it actually represents a very complex and integrated biological system.

PCA Cycle Analysis

The PCA cycle thus begins with sensing some external stimuli and normally ends by performing a physical motion or movement. If we are to better understand and improve human task performance in the workplace, then it often helps to think along the lines of the Perception–Cognition–Action cycle. If task-related human performance problems arise, for example, then a good starting point is to ask the following questions about the PCA cycle in the following sequential order (additional PCA cycle-related questions are offered in Chapter 7):

1. Was a stimulus initially detected? If not, could it have been detected via displays or some other means in the task environment or by the individual (and was that individual physically capable of detecting the presented stimulus)? If a stimulus was detected, was it detected within an adequate timeframe in which to successfully respond?
2. Was the detected stimulus correctly identified and understood? In other words, did the person(s) possess the required knowledge to identify and understand the stimulus?
3. Was a correct decision made regarding the stimulus and was a proper action selected? Did the person know what decisions could or should be made and what actions could or should be appropriately paired with each decision alternative?
4. Finally, was the selected action physically executed in a timely and accurate manner? Did the person have the requisite abilities, skills, health state, and possibly tools and enough time, to physically perform and sustain the required action?

Through many years of experience, I have found these four question sets indispensable when thinking about human performance, especially as it applies to the PCA cycle. For example, remember the finding from the *Deepwater Horizon* accident investigation described in Chapter 1 that stated, "The drilling crew and other individuals on the rig also missed critical signs that a kick was occurring. The crew could have prevented the blowout—or at least significantly reduced its impact—if they had reacted in a timely and appropriate manner."

Would not a more systematic analysis based on these four PCA cycle question sets add to the accident investigation, hopefully providing a deeper understanding of why and even possibly how the drilling crew reportedly, "... missed critical signs that a kick was occurring?" In point of fact, was it really a function of perception (of missing critical signs) or did the problem lie later in the PCA cycle? Perhaps such critical PCA cycle-related thinking would add a great deal to better understanding the human component of the *Deepwater Horizon* tragedy.

Another way to think about the PCA cycle, especially PCA-related cycle times, is via the concept of response time, as described next.

Response Time

In many instances, successful human performance entails not only doing the right thing right, but also doing the right thing right within a required timeframe. That is, completing the PCA cycle within some task-imposed time limit. As noted, one way to think about PCA cycle time is via the concept of response time.

Response time represents the length of time between the detection of a stimulus or sensory input and the completion of a motor response to that detected input. Total response time thus represents the sum of reaction time plus movement time or:

$$\text{Response Time} = \text{Reaction Time} + \text{Movement Time}$$

Reaction time is defined as the ensuing time interval between the application of a stimulus and the first indication of a physical response. Reaction time includes:

■ Perceiving or detecting a stimulus
■ Identifying and evaluating the stimulus
■ Formulating a potential response to the stimulus
■ Initiating or signaling an appropriate motor response

Using the previously presented sensing, processing, signaling, and moving model, reaction time involves sensing, processing, and neural signaling.

Associated response reactions can be either simple or choice. A *simple response reaction* requires a performer to detect only the presence of a single stimulus (e.g., detecting a "start" signal for a race). A *choice response reaction* involves making a distinct response for each class of stimuli (e.g., the ability to first identify a traffic light that has changed color and then make the correct choice as to required action).

For example, having to simply fire at a pop-up target with an assault rifle represents a simple response reaction. Sometimes, however, pop-up targets have intermixed pictures of bad and good guys (hostages) clipped to them. Bad guy targets represent shoot targets, whereas good guy targets represent no-shoot targets. In this example, the shooter has to *first* determine if it is a bad guy or good guy target, and *then* pair the appropriate response (shoot or no-shoot) to that particular target. All things being equal, choice response reactions take longer than simple response reactions.

Normally, this time difference is relatively insignificant, but sometimes it can literally determine the difference between life and death; an all too real-world worry facing police officers each time they confront a potentially armed and dangerous person. There is a golden rule in such instances and that is action is faster than reaction.

Finally, *movement time* is the defined time interval between the initiation and completion of the actual physical response. In the above pop-up target shooting example, movement time is the time required to physically aim and fire a weapon.

An important distinction between the two components comprising response time is that movement time can be physically observed, whereas reaction time can usually only be inferred. Additionally, total response time best represents a psychomotor skill or a skill comprised of both critical perceptual and cognitive parts, *and* a physical motor part. Various studies of response time suggest:

■ Generally, men have faster response times than women, especially at the college level where numerous response time experiments have been carried out.

■ There is some slight indication that left-handed people may generally have faster response times than right-handed people.

■ Younger is better. Response times often degrade with age.

■ Response time is especially important in an open motor skill environment where the performer must respond to changing conditions in the environment.

As will be described in the following section, total response times can sometimes occur literally in a fraction of a second. The presented example also provides some ideas of how one might graphically model response time (and the associated PCA cycle) for a given short-duration task. The example comes from baseball.

The Swing of a Bat

Most of us can hit a softball thrown at 30 mph in a slow-pitch baseball game. Yet, few of us possess the athletic ability to hit a fastball thrown at 92 mph by a Major League Baseball pitcher. Why is the same task—hitting a ball with a bat—so different under the two scenarios? One way to assess the difference is via required response times.

To begin this assessment, a generic input–output "hitting a baseball" response time model is developed as illustrated in Figure 3.7. Note in the diagrammed model that the initial input coming from the external environment is a pitched baseball. The final output is the swing of the bat resulting

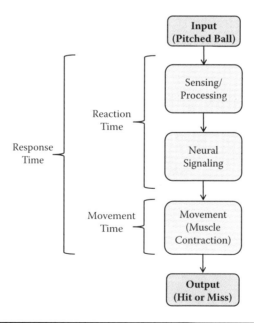

Figure 3.7   Generic input–output response time model.

in a hit or miss (strike). As further depicted, reaction time includes sensing and processing, and neural signaling. Finally, movement time involves the actual physical swing of the bat. Now, let's put some real numbers on the developed generic model depicted in Figure 3.7.

As illustrated in Figure 3.8, the distance between the pitcher and home plate in Major League Baseball is 60' 6" or 60.5 feet. A fastball pitched at 92 mph will cover that distance in approximately 448 milliseconds (ms), or a bit less than half of a second. To put this short timeframe into perspective, a blink of an eye takes approximately 300 to 400 ms.

To hit a 92-mph fastball, a batter must first detect the ball (the stimulus) after it is released from the pitcher's hand using his visual sensory acuity. Then, using his cognitive processing capabilities, he must determine (understand) the ball's trajectory, decide whether or not to swing, and if the decision is to swing, develop and initiate the required motor program. Next, the required "swing" instructions are delivered from the brain to the spinal cord (which may make those initial instructions more specific via spinal tuning) and through the peripheral nervous system to the involved muscle groups. Once those signals arrive, muscle contraction takes place and the batting movement physically commences. Hopefully, the resultant output is a hit ball.

As shown in Figure 3.8 and based on the previous generic input–output response time model developed in Figure 3.7, these various response steps can be grouped under the headings of sensing/processing, neural signaling, and movement (the actual physical swing of the bat). In this classification scheme, sensing, processing, and neural messaging represent reaction time. Movement time is represented by the physical swinging motion of the bat itself.

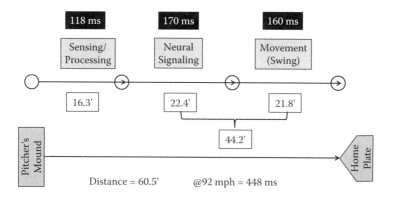

Figure 3.8 Major League Baseball batting example.

Response time is calculated by working backwards. The average measured bat swing time in the majors is about 160 ms. Neural signaling or messaging, based on experimentation, takes 170 ms. That leaves only approximately 118 ms for sensing and processing. Or to put it another way, a fastball pitched at 92 mph travels only some 16 feet (still 44 feet away from the batter) before a swing decision has to be made and initiated. Although it is certainly challenging to physically hit a baseball traveling at 92 mph, the really hard and time-constrained part of the process, as illustrated in Figure 3.8, is sensing and processing. Note also that since neural signaling and swing times are essentially fixed, pitches thrown faster than 92 mph mean even less time for sensing and processing; one reason why high-speed fastballs in excess of 97 mph have become so hard to hit in the majors.

By comparison and as depicted in Figure 3.9, the distance between the mound and home plate in slow-pitch softball is normally 50 feet. A 30-mph slow-pitched softball will travel that 50-foot distance in approximately 1,136 ms. A typical amateur bat swing takes about 175 ms. Neural signaling is the same 170 ms. This leaves 791 ms for sensing and processing. As illustrated, this much "longer" time means that the ball will travel almost 35 feet before a swing decision must be initiated. Further, the ball is only 7.7 feet away from the batter when the swing motion actually begins, making the ball much easier to hit.

So, why is hitting a 30-mph slow-pitch softball so much easier than hitting a 92-mph fastball? One very important reason is that the batter in slow-pitch softball has almost seven times longer than the Major League batter to detect the ball, determine the ball's trajectory, decide whether or not to swing, and then develop and initiate the required motor program if the decision is to swing. That is, the design of the task itself is

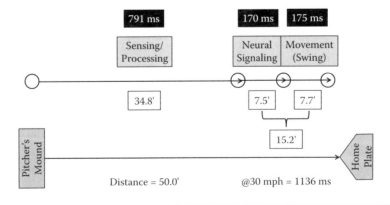

Figure 3.9 Slow-pitch softball batting example.

decidedly different and, therefore, considerably easier. Those extra 673 ms (791 ms – 118 ms), representing some two blinks of an eye, apparently make all the difference in the world. Indeed as described earlier, in order to hit a 92-mph fastball pitch requires not only a greater level of athletic ability and skill than that possessed by the average person, but apparently some very unique biologically endowed characteristics as well, including possessing almost extraordinary visual acuity or eyesight.

A key take-away point from this baseball example is that sometimes making even relatively minor, "two blinks of an eye" improvements in a task can have a disproportionate effect on improving human performance. In this example, that minor increase in time meant going from an almost "nobody can do it" task, to an almost "everyone can do it" task.

In summary, human performance at the individual task level involves perception, cognition, and action. This highly integrated PCA cycle, in turn, requires sensing, mental processing, neural signaling, and physical movement. Problems in individual performance at the elemental task level often involve some problem with perception, cognition, and/or action. Better understanding the role that the PCA cycle plays in facilitating human performance represents a critical first step in improving performance.

Chapter 4

Human Error (or Is It Really?)

Success *and* failure are emergent properties of essentially any work system. As such, they may be viewed as opposite sides of the same system-related performance coin, separated sometimes by a much narrower rim or margin than we might first think. In order to begin to understand work system failure (as often evidenced by a catastrophic accident or a costly quality problem), it is imperative that we better understand the role that human performance and human error play in failure. Successfully achieving this better understanding is critical if we are to prevent or at least negate the almost always costly and sometimes tragic consequences of failure.

Many industries grapple with work system-related failure. As previously noted, in many instances, such failures are attributed wholly or at least partially to human or "pilot error." Some industries seem especially plagued by human error, including the medical industry. According to an analysis of medical errors published in a December 20, 2012 *Wall Street Journal* article, surgeons make over 4,000 preventable mistakes each year. These mistakes range from leaving objects inside patients to operating on the wrong body part to even worse, occasionally operating on the wrong patient altogether.

In one study, as described in the *Wall Street Journal* article, researchers identified 9,744 "never event" cases between 1990 and 2010. "Never events" represent the kinds of mistakes that should never happen in medicine. As a result of these never-should-happen mistakes:

- 6 percent of the patients died
- 32.9 percent had some permanent injury
- 59.2 percent suffered temporary injury

Surgical-related "never" mistake causal percentages included:

- 49.8 percent involved leaving a foreign object behind in a patient (left-behind surgical sponges seemed particularly prevalent and sometimes simply stayed inside a patient, never to be discovered or removed).
- 25.1 percent involved performing a wrong surgical procedure on a patient.
- 24.8 percent involved performing a supposedly "right" surgical procedure, but on the wrong body part.
- 0.3 percent involved operating on the wrong patient altogether.

Obviously, such surgical errors have potentially catastrophic consequences, especially if you are unlucky enough to be the affected patient. But how are we to begin tackling this seemingly vexing "human error" problem, particularly when so many people (especially so many managers) view the role of human performance and human error so differently? I personally discovered these stark differences in human error attitudes quite early in my human performance-oriented career.

An Early Experience

After earning a PhD in Applied Behavioral Studies, my first job out of graduate school was working as a research scientist in a human factors group at a Department of Energy national laboratory. Besides conducting human performance-related research, I also served as a human performance specialist on a Nuclear Regulatory Commission (NRC) incident investigation team (but working only in a consulting role to the NRC).

Whenever there was some type of incident or event at a public utility nuclear power plant, our team was required to be onsite within 24 hours following the event to begin a formal investigation. Actual onsite time during these investigations normally lasted some four to five days. Prior to leaving the power plant following an investigation, the team always held a formal out-brief meeting with the utility's upper-level management. The purpose of the out-brief meeting was to share our team's initial findings, which were later refined and converted into a final NRC report.

I remember vividly one such out-brief meeting. A rather serious radioactive contamination incident had occurred (to be described in greater detail later in this chapter). As the meeting began, a senior manager from the utility pronounced three definite "facts" as a result of the company's own internal and parallel investigation:

1. The odds of such an event happening were at least one in a million, if not one in 10 million—an almost statistical improbability.
2. The "root cause" of the incident was human error—plain and simple.
3. As a result of those human errors, the "perpetrators" of the errors would be disciplined. Disciplinary actions could include dismissal for some control room personnel.

The night before the out-brief meeting, I had jotted down a few observations as well. My initial findings, however, were decidedly different, and included:

■ Based on back-of-the-envelope calculations using a human reliability assessment methodology, I calculated that the odds of the incident occurring at an almost unbelievable one in three or even one in two number—statistically, an almost sure thing.
■ The particular tasks being performed and associated task demands and task setting contributed to creating an almost insurmountable set of error-producing conditions. These identified error-producing conditions contributed to setting up involved personnel to fail almost from the outset of the performed operation.
■ Management should certainly not discipline those personnel involved in the incident. Rather, management needed to better understand how initial task design and associated task-related environmental factors can sometimes lead to unwanted outcomes. Additionally, they should take proactive measures in future complex task iterations to prevent similar reoccurrences of the just experienced incident.

After departing the site, I never did learn what happened to those identified human error offenders. However, the incident does point out the often contrasting views regarding the whole subject of human error. A few of these divergent views are discussed next.

Differing Views

Some authors describe differing human error-related views under the headings of "old view" and "new view." Under this "old view" view, which in many ways still remains the current view in numerous organizations, human error is viewed as a *cause* of failure, especially when those failures lead to an accident. For example, one U.S. General Accounting Office report noted that "… Our investigation revealed human error to be the primary cause of the … incident."

Under this old view paradigm, if we are to explain failure, then we must seek out and identify those humans who are responsible for the failure. That is, we must place blame (and often shame). Or, as Dekker (2002) notes, we must discover people's "… inaccurate assessments, wrong decisions, deviations from the rules, and bad judgments."

I find when adapting this old view perspective, many managers follow these four steps in their precise order:

1. They immediately identify a simple and single root cause that is deemed "responsible" for the incident.
2. They then identify, blame, shame, and often punish those onerous villains who caused the incident.
3. They also often blame, shame, and punish the supervisors and next-level managers of the offenders identified in Step #2.
4. And, above all else, they do absolutely nothing to understand the overall context of the incident or how that work system-related context may have actually led to the identified human errors.

Admittedly, there are some distinct advantages in following this four-step procedure. It is simple, fast, and requires little investigation or deeper thought. It also makes the head guy or gal of an organization appear tough on combating human error. Unfortunately, it does little if anything to improve work system performance, especially associated human performance.

I also think that one of the major fallacies in this old view of human error is the incorrect presumption that accidents must always have a single or primary cause of failure. We seem to intuitively seek that single cause, which often involves finding someone or more than one person to personally blame for the unwanted event. For example, in a nuclear industry-related website that I follow, a person recently wanted to know the most important root cause of the Japanese Fukushima nuclear disaster. In truth, such a "most important root cause" rarely, if ever exists. Instead, a network of causes occur in an often complex and highly interdependent and interactive manner.

Fortunately, there is also a new and evolving view of human error. Some people even call it going "beyond human error." This new view portends that human performance is very much shaped by work system *context* (the same concept as presented in Chapter 2). Within this new, context-centric framework, if we are to truly understand human performance and why humans perform in a certain way, including making errors, then we first must understand the work setting context—the tools, tasks, and associated environmental task factors—in which human performance takes place.

Remember Dekker's (2002) astute observation that the real point in learning about human error is not to find out where people went wrong, rather, it is to find out why their assessments and actions (even supposedly wrong ones) made sense to them at the time. That is, we must attempt to truly understand the context of an event and how that context affected human decision making and subsequent human actions. Although we humans certainly make errors, we rarely do so purposely or in a malicious manner.

In a fictional work, authors Preston and Child (2001) make a rather perceptive observation when they note that a certain company "… realized long ago that the key to understanding failure was understanding exactly how human beings made mistakes." Accordingly, this need to better understand how humans make mistakes, especially in relation to work system context, is explored more fully in subsequent sections. However, before leaving this current section, it may prove helpful to point out some of the thoughts offered by Atul Gawande regarding human error.

According to Gawande (2009), whose primary interest is in medical errors, it is important to understand the difference between ignorance and ineptitude. *Ignorance* means not knowing something. *Ineptitude* involves applying "known" knowledge incorrectly. Gawande points out that failures of "… ignorance we commonly forgive. Failures of ineptitude we commonly don't forgive." In our usage, a failure of ineptitude represents some type of human error, which as Gawande properly points out, is rarely forgiven.

Gawande further observes that the capability of individuals "… is not proving to be our primary difficulty, whether in medicine or elsewhere." Rather, Gawande argues that "getting the steps 'right' is proving brutally hard, even if we know them." That is, we often know what to do, but we do not always do that "what to do" for a number of differing reasons.

Referring back to those "never should happen" surgical errors, half involved leaving a foreign object behind in a patient and the other half involved either performing a "wrong" surgical procedure on a right patient or performing the right procedure on the "wrong" body part. At first, all of these errors appear to be amazingly simple stuff and intuitively obvious. Upon closer examination, however, all the identified surgical errors involve either forgetting a critical task step, or executing what would seem to be at least an obvious step incorrectly (like operating on the right body part).

Thus "getting the steps right" is certainly a big part of improving human performance. However, that step-related part must be framed within better understanding of the concept of system context and how context can positively or negatively affect getting those critical steps right. This important work system context-related topic is explored next.

Work System Context

Sometimes under the right conditions, simple mistakes and systemic organizational weaknesses combine with deadly consequences. For example, one tragic airplane accident that occurred at an Asian airport involved:

■ *Right conditions*: An extremely dark, rainy, and wet night caused by an approaching typhoon.
■ *Simple mistakes*: The pilot turned onto and attempted to take off from a closed runway that was under repair.
■ *Systemic organizational weaknesses*: The closed runway was poorly and improperly marked (i.e., lighted incorrectly).

Note in the above example how a multitude of factors or "context" conspired to create an unwanted and deadly outcome: an approaching typhoon, a wrong turn, and an improperly marked runway. One way to think about system context—about simple mistakes and systemic organizational weaknesses—is via the concept of latent and active factors (also commonly termed *latent* and *active errors*).

At any given time, a particular causal factor in an adverse event can be either latent or active. Latent means present, but not active. Active means the factor is present and is currently "occurring."

Latent factors are those "setup" factors present before an adverse event occurs. Note later in this chapter, that the concept of *error-producing conditions* is introduced. As described, such conditions negatively affect human reliability (i.e., human performance). In my usage, an error-producing condition represents a particular type of human performance-related latent factor.

Latent factors induce vulnerability into a system. They also make a system more "error prone" for sometimes unsuspecting and fallible humans. In the above aircraft example, the poorly and improperly marked closed runway is classified as a latent factor.

Active factors are those triggering, forcing, or initiating factors. Human error is a common active factor. Incorrectly turning onto the poorly and improperly marked closed runway in the above example represents an active factor—a human error.

Think of a buried landmine as representing a latent factor. It is present, but by itself, is not causing any immediate harm (although it very well has the potential to cause harm). Physically stepping on the landmine is an active factor. Accordingly, in many instances, active factors are needed to literally "trigger" passive and sometimes deeply buried latent factors in a work system. A key point is that if we can successfully remove latent factors from a system, then there is nothing to be triggered by active errors (e.g., there are no landmines to physically step on). This is one important way to make a work system more tolerant to the effects of human error.

Some research suggests that in an unwanted event, active factors represent 30 percent of the pie chart, whereas latent factors represent a whopping 70 percent (see Figure 4.1). Yet, unfortunately, in analyzing an adverse incident, we often focus only on identifying active factors; the 30 percent of the pie chart. This myopic focus normally results in gaining only a very limited understanding of the event itself, with few useable lessons learned. In such incomplete analyses, we frequently set ourselves up for a more-or-less repeat of a similar event.

During graduate school, a professor of mine once told an interesting story about the relationship between latent and active factors. I am not sure if the story is even true, but I think it is worth repeating here

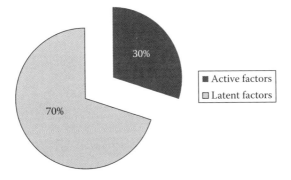

Figure 4.1 Estimated percentages of active and latent factors.

nonetheless because it is such a great example. Supposedly, the event took place at a satellite control station located outside of Moscow, Russia. It is in the middle of a cold Siberian night (the graveyard shift) when a Soviet-era satellite begins passing over the station. A supervisor orders a technician to input and send a minor adjustment command to the overhead orbiting satellite.

The supervisor and technician are waiting for the sent command to reach the satellite when all of a sudden the satellite disappears from the technician's tracking screen. It turns out that while the technician was supposed to enter the minor adjustment command "X247865WTZ," he instead transposed two numbers and incorrectly entered the code as "X247685WTX."

This wrongly entered code was unfortunately the self-destruct code. Supposedly, after entering the incorrect code, there were no follow-on queries, such as: Do you really want to blow up the satellite? Do you really, really want to blow up the satellite? – Dammit, you are about to blow up the satellite!

Note in this case how the unsuspecting technician literally tripped over an embedded landmine or flawed latent error previously engineered into the system. Also note that this active error—transposing two numbers—is a fairly high probability-occurring error. We have all transposed two numbers while entering numerical data into a spreadsheet, for example, and we will certainly continue to do so. In point of fact, we really cannot prevent these types of errors from occurring. Thus, in this satellite-related example, a high probability active or human error was just waiting to trip over a potentially harmful, embedded latent error.

This high probability transposition error occurrence brings up an important point regarding human error in general. In truth, human error cannot be entirely eliminated. At best, it can only be somewhat reduced (and even then, only sometimes). I once heard a human performance improvement specialist in a training class state that human performance improvement is all about *eliminating* human errors. That unfortunately is not true and is essentially impossible to achieve. Although we can sometimes eliminate an unwanted "consequence" associated with a human error (more about this in Chapter 8), and we can certainly identify and remove latent factors from the work setting, making it more error tolerant, we really cannot eliminate all human errors per se. Making human errors is, well, human.

About as good as it gets in what are called *Human Error Probabilities* is one in a thousand. This one in a thousand figure means that humans commonly make an error in at least every 1,000 opportunities to do so (although that number is often a much lower "one in a hundred" or even "one in ten" figure). But even knowing that we cannot completely eliminate human error from the workplace, there are still many positive things that we can do. One of those positive things that we can do is to better understand how poorly designed work systems loaded with embedded latent factor landmines can adversely affect human performance.

Before leaving this latent and active factor discussion, a case study might be illustrative. Although the presented case study involving the capsizing of the *MS Herald of Free Enterprise* is a bit dated (the accident occurred on March 6, 1987), it still remains a classic incident and continues to be well worth studying. The tragic event, which claimed 193 lives, clearly demonstrates the earlier observation that under the right conditions, simple mistakes (now called active factors or errors) and systemic organizational weaknesses (termed latent factors) can sometimes combine with deadly consequences.

MS Herald of Free Enterprise

In the early evening of March 6, 1987, the roll-on, roll-off *MS Herald of Free Enterprise*, a modern eight-deck car and passenger ferry, prepared to depart Zeebrugge Harbor in Belgium. The loaded ferry was bound for Dover, England. When it left its berth in the inner harbor that night, it was carrying a reported compliment of 80 crew, 459 passengers, 81 cars, 47 trucks, and 3 buses.

Prior to its departure (~1800 Greenwich Meridian Time or GMT), the assistant bosun failed to close the forward bow doors after the last harbor station call, per his assigned task. The bow doors were left open as the ferry prepared to depart the inner harbor.

At around 1805 GMT, just prior to departure, the first officer failed to ensure that the bow doors were secured prior to leaving port. Consequently, the bow doors remained open as the ferry departed the protected inner harbor.

The captain of the vessel increased speed after passing the outer mole or breakwater at approximately 1815 GMT. It was always assumed by the captain that the bow doors had been safely secured unless he was told otherwise. In this instance, although the captain assumed the bow doors were closed, a routine assumption he commonly made, they, in fact, still remained open.

At approximately 1825 GMT, bow waves began to rise above the upper hull, causing water to flow along the main car deck through the still opened bow doors. Almost immediately (~1826 GMT), the large ferry became unstable. It capsized approximately one minute later (~1827 GMT).

Fortunately, because the ferry was so near the harbor and still in shallow water at the time it capsized, numerous rescue boats were able to quickly reach the scene of the overturned ship. This quick reaction undoubtedly saved countless lives. However, even with this quick and heroic rescue response effort, the death toll still amounted to 193 lost passengers and crew members.

To better understand exactly what happened on that fateful night, the following approximate chronology has been reconstructed:

~1730 GMT: The ferry's bosun releases the assistant bosun from duty, who returns to his cabin and immediately falls asleep. He fails to awaken prior to the last harbor station call.

~1800 GMT: The off-duty assistant bosun, still asleep, fails to close the bow doors after the last harbor station call, per his assigned task. The doors are left open.

~1805 GMT: The first officer "thinks" he saw the assistant bosun going to close the bow doors. However, he does not personally ensure that the bow doors are secured when leaving port, per requirement. The bow doors remain open.

~1815 GMT: The captain increases speed after passing the outer mole, unaware of the still opened bow doors. The captain cannot see the bow doors from the bridge. Because of this inability, he has requested multiple times for a bow door status indicator light to be installed on the bridge. Management, however, has repeatedly refused his requests. Additionally, it is standard practice to assume that the bow doors are closed, unless they are reported to be open. Unfortunately, this standard use of negative information can inadvertently set up a very dangerous situation, especially if both the assistant bosun *and* the first officer fail to perform their required bow door-related duties. These various combinations and resultant success and failure outcomes regarding the use of negative information are analyzed more fully in Figure 4.2.

~1825 GMT: Bow waves rise above the lower hull. The ship is trimmed with its bow in a slightly downward tilt of 0.8 meters. Past requests for better ballast pumps to properly trim the vessel are refused by management due to the high costs of the pumps.

Assistant Bosun	First Officer	Ship's Captain	Ship Condition
Closes bow doors.	Ensures bow doors are closed.	Assumes bow doors are closed.	Safe
Fails to close bow doors.	Detects bow doors still remain open.	Made aware that bow doors are still open.	Safe
Closes bow doors.	Fails to ensure bow doors are closed.	Assumes bow doors are closed.	Safe
Fails to close bow doors.	Fails to ensure bow doors are closed.	Assumes bow doors are closed.	Unsafe

Figure 4.2   Negative information analysis.

~1825+ GMT: Water begins to flow onto the main car deck. There are no subdividing bulkheads present on the ship to prevent main car deck flooding.

~1826 GMT: The ferry becomes unstable and almost immediately capsizes.

Based on this brief analysis, the following active and latent factors are identified:

■ Active Factors
  - Assistant bosun fails to close bow doors per requirement.
  - First officer fails to ensure bow doors are closed per requirement.
  - Captain increases speed at outer mole unaware that bow doors remained open (this increase in speed immediately causes waves to rise above the bow).
■ Latent Factors
  - The use of negative information; it is standard procedure to assume bow doors are closed if not reported open.
  - Captain cannot see bow doors from the bridge, therefore, cannot independently verify their status.
  - No bow door indicator light is present on the bridge to independently display bow door status (despite repeated requests for the installation of such an indicator light).

- HFE is always trimmed at the bow, making it more susceptible to flooding from the front.
- No subdividing bulkheads present to prevent flooding across main car decks.

Admittedly to some extent, this is an example of human failure. The assistant bosun was asleep when he should have been working (however, we do not know if this was caused by excess fatigue or some other medical condition). Also, the chief officer failed to verify that the bow doors were secured per standard operating procedure (once again, we do not know exactly why).

Yet if some of the latent factors had been removed, especially if a bow door status indicator light had been installed on the bridge, the odds of this accident happening would have been considerably reduced. Although, in the exact described scenario, the same active factors or errors would have been committed by the assistant bosun and first officer, those errors, and the open bow doors, would have probably been caught by the captain via the bow door indicator light *before* the vessel departed the inner harbor. Or, in other words, although the human errors would still have occurred, there would have likely been no associated adverse consequence associated with those errors, represented here by the capsizing of the ferry. Accordingly, and as previously stated, one way to significantly improve a work system is to eliminate adverse consequences caused by probable human errors by eliminating system-embedded latent factors.

Additionally, something that the captain could have done immediately was to discontinue the practice of "negative information" or always assuming that the bow doors were closed unless told otherwise. In a new "positive information" redesigned work system, the first officer would have had to verbally confirm to the captain that the bow doors had been secured. Although this proposed redesign is not an absolute guarantee that the bow doors could still not be left open, it would have significantly reduced the probability that they would remain open.

Admittedly, this proposed work system redesign would probably add some "psychological distance" to the task of ensuring that the bow doors were always secured prior to leaving port. However, in this particular case and without a bridge-mounted bow door status indicator light, that added psychological distance is worth the trouble, despite the increased hassle factor.

Certainly much has improved in maritime safety and ferry vessel construction in general in the 27 years since the sinking of the *MS Herald of*

Free Enterprise. Yet, perhaps a bit ironically, as I write this chapter, a large South Korean ferry named the *Sewol* lies capsized in the shallow waters off the coast of South Korea. Images of the overturned vessel are eerily similar to earlier images taken of the capsized *MS Herald of Free Enterprise.* To date, 293 bodies have been recovered from the overturned South Korean ferry, with divers continuing to search for an additional 11 passengers who still remain missing. Tragically, many of the dead and missing passengers are young teenagers, all from the same high school traveling together on a school-sponsored field trip.

According to some early reports (yet to be verified), the captain of the vessel reported carrying 150 cars and 657 tons of "other cargo." However, an executive from the company that loaded the other cargo claimed that 3,608 tons of cargo was loaded onboard the ferry, more than three times the authorized loading limit of the *Sewol.* Some suggest that a sharp and unexpected turn of the ferry (reason unknown) caused this massive and unauthorized amount of cargo to shift, resulting in the vessel's almost immediate capsizing.

As I have studied major accidents over the years and have developed various in-depth case studies of some of those accidents, I have come to think of such events as somewhat akin to Shakespearian plays. Although the actors performing Shakespearian characters certainly change from play to play, the themes of the plays stay basically the same. And, so it seems with many accidents—the themes or patterns stay constant. As such, the more some things change, the more other things, like unwanted accidents, stay the same.

As illustrated in this maritime-related case study, humans certainly do make mistakes. However, what exactly is human error? This topic is explored next.

Human Error

The formal definition of *human error* is rather complex. It is defined as:

■ Unintended actions or inactions that arise from problems in:
  – Task sequencing
  – Timing
  – Knowledge
  – Interfaces, and/or
  – Procedures

- That result in deviations from expected standards or norms
- That place people, equipment, and systems at risk

Based on this definition of "unintended actions or inactions," human errors are further classified under the headings of errors of omission and errors of commission. An *error of omission* involves inadvertently omitting or not performing a required task step (forgetting to do something, for whatever reason). *Errors of commission* involve performing a required action incorrectly (you do it, but you do it in a wrong manner).

Some examples of errors of omission include:

- Four fasteners were not installed while reattaching an elevon hydraulic actuator to a local wing structure.
- A pneumatic duct was not reconnected following a routine maintenance procedure.
- A surgeon did not remove a surgical sponge following a lengthy operation.
- Closed valves were not reopened following a maintenance activity.
- Electricians failed to remove grounding plugs prior to reenergizing a transformer.
- A "remove before flight" tape was left on a connector prior to flight.
- Plumbers did not relight a pilot light on a hot water tank after completing the installation of new plumbing.
- Cockpit circuit breakers were not reset after the rear rotor was repaired.

Examples of errors of commission include:

- Gyroscope axes were improperly switched in a flight control system.
- Hoses, which supplied compressed air to rotate a valve to the "open" or "closed" positions, were improperly reversed when reconnected.
- A direct-broadcasting satellite was launched with its antennas improperly wired: horizontal was wired to vertical and vertical was wired to horizontal.
- The "right" operation was performed on the wrong body part.
- Just prior to launch, the paddles used to stir liquid oxygen in a tank had been bench tested. However, during installation, the paddles had been reconnected to the wrong power supply.

As illustrated by these varied real-world examples, errors of omission involve omitting or not doing something that is required, such as not reconnecting a pneumatic duct following a routine aircraft maintenance operation. By contrast, errors of commission involve doing something, but doing it incorrectly, such as wiring horizontal to vertical and vertical to horizontal.

Thinking in terms of the previously described Perception–Cognition–Action (PCA) cycle, errors of omission mostly involve some failure of not sensing or detecting something (literally out of sight means out of mind) and/or problems with cognition (forgetting something). Likewise, errors of commission also commonly involve some problem with either perception and/or cognition. Some specific techniques for combating these "sensing and remembering" issues are offered in Chapter 8.

Errors of commission can be analyzed on a finer scale, especially at the discrete, individual microstep level. Completing many tasks (e.g., maintenance, surgery, etc.) involves performing:

- *Actions* on
- *Objects* at specified
- *Locations* using
- *Resources* to some required or inferred
- *Condition* or *specification*.

For example, the task to "manually turn valve at station 211 to the open position" can be dissected in the following manner:

- Manually (the *resource* or "tool")
- Turn (the *action*)
- Valve (the *object*)
- At station 211 (the *location*)
- To the open position (*condition* or *specification*).

Similarly, the task, "visually inspect pipe at bend for cracking," also can be dissected in the same way:

- Visually (the *resource*)
- Inspect (the *action*)
- Pipe (the *object*)
- At bend (*location*)
- For cracking (*condition* or *specification*).

Based on this type of discrete, microstep analysis, an error of commission can be "caused" by performing the wrong action with the wrong object at the wrong location using the wrong resource at the wrong specification. In many instances, errors of commission involve the wrong object or the wrong location. For example, consider the following incidences of errors of commission once again:

■ Gyroscope axes were improperly switched in a flight control system.
■ A direct-broadcasting satellite was launched with its antennas improperly wired: horizontal was wired vertical and vertical was wired horizontal.
■ The "right" operation was performed on the wrong body part.
■ Just prior to launch, the paddles used to stir liquid oxygen in a tank had been bench tested. However, during installation, the paddles had been reconnected to the wrong power supply.

In each of these examples, either the "right" object was connected to the "wrong" location, or the "wrong" object was connected to the "right" location. In the case of the surgical error, the "right action" was performed at the wrong location. Unfortunately, there is not enough specific information in the above error descriptions to determine if the problem involved selecting the wrong object or the wrong location. That is why it is often necessary to delve deeper to truly understand either an error of omission or an error of commission; in this case, the devil (or reason) is truly in the details.

In some instances, human errors occur in a fairly predictable place or order in a task sequence. This "predictable place" observation has been especially well documented in the aviation maintenance field. However, the same findings have broad applicability to other fields and industries as well, especially the medical industry.

In point of fact, I am always a bit surprised when I read an employment ad for a human performance improvement specialist in the medical field. Such ads seem to require past medical or hospital experience. Personally, if I were to hire a human performance specialist to work in a hospital setting, I would much prefer someone that came from the worlds of aviation maintenance, nuclear power generation, or nuclear weapon maintenance or dismantlement; worlds in which the study of human error are much farther advanced.

Human errors in maintenance can lead to immediate or latent unsafe conditions that, in turn, can sometimes have catastrophic consequences. There is a saying in the aviation industry that pilots are the ones who normally deal with maintenance errors.

Figure 4.3 depicts the maintenance process, beginning with initial planning and ending with "egress" following the completion of a maintenance task. Most human errors occur in the repair–service–install part of the process.

As illustrated in Figure 4.4, the repair–service–install activity often entails the *deactivation* and *disassembly* of components and their subsequent reassembly, reconfiguration, and reactivation.

Unfortunately, the latter activities of reassembly, reconfiguration, and reactivation often involve errors. James Reason, author of *Human Error* (1990) and co-author of *Managing Maintenance Error* along with Alan Hobbs (2003), is a recognized expert in maintenance-related human

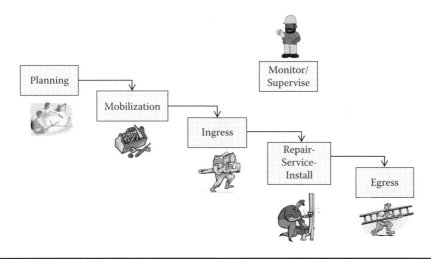

Figure 4.3 General maintenance process.

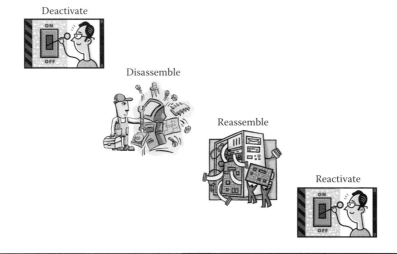

Figure 4.4 Repair–service–install process activity.

factors issues. Reason observes that reassembly, reconfiguration, and reactivation tasks represent intrinsically error prone activities.

When identifying error types associated with the reassembly, reinstallation, restoration, and reactivation of components, errors of omission comprise the single largest category. For example, in a survey of one major airline, errors of omission accounted for nearly 60 percent of all recorded maintenance lapses, as charted in Figure 4.5. I also have added to the bar chart in Figure 4.5 surgical-related "never should happen" medical errors as described in the introduction of this chapter. Note here that the split between surgical-related errors of omission and commission is essentially 50/50.

A key point in such analyses is that the specific task step that eventually led to the later error of omission often occurs *much earlier* in the overall task sequence. Further, this earlier step is often physically not associated with a primary "ending" task step. For example, in the error of omission involving a pneumatic duct not being reconnected, the pneumatic duct was disconnected much earlier in the aircraft maintenance procedure. Additionally, the bulk of the maintenance procedure involved working on a whole different part of the plane from where the pneumatic duct was located.

Similarly, surgical sponges are often placed inside a patient much earlier in an operating procedure. Their subsequent removal is not directly related to the final action of stitching the patient back together at the end of an operation. That is, surgeons can physically "end" an operation without removing earlier inserted surgical sponges.

Likewise, when electricians failed to remove grounding plugs prior to reenergizing a newly installed transformer, those grounding plugs had been installed many days earlier prior to performing the final task step of

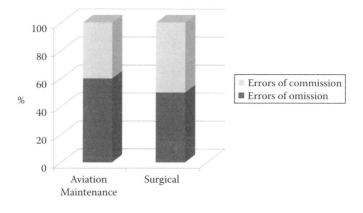

Figure 4.5 Aircraft maintenance and surgical-related error percentages.

reenergizing the transformer. Of special note is that the electricians who failed to remove the grounding plugs prior to reenergizing the transformer had been reminded about the grounding plugs in an early morning prejob briefing on the final day that they were to reenergize the transformer. However, the actual step of removing the grounding plugs did not occur until some 10 hours later at the end of a very exhausting and busy day. How many times, for example, have you been told to do something first thing in the morning, only to forget it after a very long and busy day?

Finally, when workers failed to relight the pilot light on a hot water tank, that pilot light was extinguished early in the morning while they worked on plumbing in a whole different part of the house for the remainder of the day. Completing the "other part of the house" plumbing job and relighting the pilot light (which was located in the basement) were separate and physically disconnected work activities.

In each instance, the pneumatic duct, surgical sponges, grounding plugs, and hot water tank were literally out of sight and, consequently, out of mind. One way to deal with errors of omission, especially those "out of sight" errors involving successfully completing a final and unrelated task step, is to provide what Reason and Hobbs (2003) call "good reminders." General characteristics and examples of good reminders are discussed more fully in Chapter 8.

As described, in many instances the occurrence of errors of omission and errors of commission are exacerbated by work system context, especially the presence of unwanted, human-related latent factors or so-called error-producing conditions—a topic discussed next.

Error-Producing Conditions

By way of introducing this last subject in the chapter, it may prove helpful to revisit the nuclear power plant incident that I briefly mentioned in the chapter's introduction. While conducting a *nonroutine test*, a command was inadvertently given in the plant's control room to floor personnel working in a sub-basement to open one valve before the closing of another valve was completed. This unintended action resulted in the release of radioactively contaminated water into a confined area within the sub-basement, and a slight injury and contamination to one person working in that sub-basement area. Although the release of the radioactively contaminated water was confined to the immediate building, it still necessitated a time-consuming and costly cleanup effort.

As noted in the introduction, following the incident, management personnel expressed genuine surprise that the event had occurred. After initially investigating the incident, they thought that it was merely a case of "operator error" and a one in a million, if not greater, improbable event.

Yet our investigation of the event identified a number of error-producing conditions that led up to the incident. These identified error-producing conditions included:

■ Workers were performing a very complex, knowledge-based cognitive task in parallel with another task.
■ The complex, nonroutine task had never been performed in this exact same manner before.
■ Displays in the control room provided inadequate feedback as to valve status (i.e., they did not indicate if valves were actually open or closed).
■ Because of the uniqueness of the nonroutine test, personnel were inexperienced in its execution.
■ All personnel were highly fatigued. One key control room individual, for example, had been working approximately 17 hours at the time of the incident.
■ There were high associated levels of stress among control room personnel conducting the test. At the time of the incident, the test sequence was behind schedule and considerable pressure was being exerted by management to complete the test "now."

Reviewing this extended list of error-producing conditions, is it really any wonder that the incident occurred? Now knowing about these error-producing conditions that were present, would you believe that the odds of the event happening were one in a million, if not greater? I did not at the time of the investigation, either.

I think an important lesson that can be learned from this incident is that some tasks and/or task settings (the context) are by their very nature more prone to inducing human errors than other tasks and associated task settings. That is, they sometimes contain potentially dangerous error-producing conditions. Accordingly, by proactively identifying and removing error-producing conditions (or more preferably, not creating them in the first place), the probability (but admittedly not certainty) of making an unwanted human error can be reduced, sometimes significantly so.

But, how can we systematically go about identifying and removing error-producing conditions from the work setting? Fortunately, one tool that I have found extremely useful for such "hunt and destroy" missions was developed by Jeremy Williams (1988). It is named the Human Error Assessment and Reduction Technique or HEART. Williams initially developed his human error assessment technique for the nuclear power industry. It was to be used as an aid when performing human reliability analyses. It was further fashioned to assist in the cost-effective design of power plants, and also to support operational performance decision making. The good news about HEART is that it can be applied to essentially any work setting. Consequently, it has relevance and value across differing industries.

Some of the basic premises underlying HEART include:

■ Human reliability is dependent upon the generic nature of the task being performed. Reliability refers to consistency. The opposite of reliability is variability. For example, one reason why you probably continue to frequent a particular restaurant is because it is reliable—regarding both the quality of the service and the food. High human reliability implies that task performance is conducted in a consistent, high quality, accurate, and safe manner. Specifically, human reliability is the probability that the performance of a person or group of people will be successful. Achieving high human reliability is a function of possessing requisite individual abilities and skills, *and* a positive work context. For example, if you are about to undergo a surgical procedure, then you definitely want an able and skilled surgeon, and a high-performance surgical work context.

■ Given "perfect" task conditions, a certain level of high reliability will tend to be consistently achieved with a given nominal likelihood within probabilistic limits. In other words, there is a high certainty (bounded by statistical limits) that performance of the task will be performed correctly and an associated outcome is successful.

■ Given that these "perfect" task conditions do not always exist in all circumstances, human reliability probabilities previously predicted may be expected to *degrade* as a function of the extent to which identified error-producing conditions are present. This premise is important and at the core or "heart" of the HEART methodology. The extent, number, and severity of error-producing conditions have the potential to degrade human reliability and, by association, overall human performance. Or, in other words, because of the presence of error-producing conditions, a so-called "perfect' task setting can be degraded to an "imperfect" setting, one that may greatly facilitate human error.

Some other important attributes of error-producing conditions as described by Williams include:

■ Error-producing conditions are predicted only to lower human reliability. They can never improve it. Therefore, embedded error-producing conditions will never make human performance "better" or increase the probability of successful task performance. They only make matters worse.

■ A multitude or greater number of error-producing conditions lead to ever further reductions in human performance reliability. When it comes to error-producing conditions, more is not better.

■ Error-producing conditions have generally consistent effects on human reliability and, therefore, are not task specific. Consequently, an error-producing condition can have the same negative effect on a hospital setting that it can in the control room of a nuclear power plant or on an assembly line at an auto plant. This is why HEART-identified error-producing conditions have such broad application across differing work settings. People are essentially affected by error-producing conditions in the exact same manner.

According to Williams, an error-producing condition or "source" of human unreliability can have a varying strength of effect. Remember, all effects are negative, some just more negative than others. For example, impaired system knowledge can have a very great negative effect on human performance. Response time shortages also can have a great negative effect if the system is unforgiving, and poor or ambiguous system feedback can have a strong negative effect.

The HEART methodology was originally designed to be used in a quantitative fashion when assessing human reliability. However, I have found that subjectively sorting the various identified error-producing conditions under the categories of *very strong negative effect*, *strong negative effect*, and *moderate to low negative effect* is much easier for the applied human performance improvement practitioner or others who really do not want to get into the statistical or mathematical part of the HEART methodology.

Using this more subjective approach, all one has to do is qualitatively add up the number of identified error-producing conditions at the end of the analysis to get some feel as to the robustness or reliability (or more often the "unreliability") of a given task setting. Although admittedly such a subjective approach lacks a more quantitative basis behind it, it nevertheless provides a quick appraisal of the possible robustness of a particular work setting.

Based on this derived sorting technique, I identify HEART error-producing conditions under the following three categories (note the corresponding number in parentheses implies the degree of negative effect on human reliability or its error-producing "power"):

Very strong negative effect
1. Unfamiliarity with a situation that is potentially important, but which only occurs infrequently or which is novel (x17).
2. A shortage of time available for error detection and correction (x11).
3. A low signal-to-noise ratio (x10).

Strong negative effect
4. A means of suppressing or over-riding information of features is too easily accessible (x9).
5. No means of conveying spatial and functional information to operators, which they can readily assimilate, such as caused by bad visual displays (x8).
6. A mismatch between an operator's mental model of the world and that imagined by the designer (x8).
7. No obvious means of reversing an unintended action (x8).
8. A channel capacity overload, particularly one caused by presentation of nonredundant information (x6).
9. A need to unlearn a technique and apply one that requires the application of an opposing philosophy (6).

Moderate to lower negative effect
10. The need to transfer specific knowledge from task to task without loss (5.5).
11. Ambiguity in task-required performance standards (x5).
12. A mismatch between perceived and real risk (x4).
13. Poor, ambiguous, or ill-matched system feedback (x4).
14. No clear direct and timely confirmation of an intended action from the portion of the system over which control is exerted (x4).
15. Operator inexperience (x3).

16. An impoverished quality of information conveyed by procedures and person-to-person interaction (x3).
17. Little or no independent checking or testing of output (x3).
18. Task objectives in conflict (x2.5).
19. Lack of diversity in task-related information sources (x2.5).
20. Personnel educational and training mismatch (x2).
21. Dangerous reward system; getting it done versus getting it done safely (x2).
22. Lack of adequate rest breaks (x1.8).
23. Unreliable instruments (x1.6).
24. Required judgments outside of operator's knowledge, training, and/or experience (x1.6).
25. Unclear allocation of job responsibilities and functions (x1.6).
26. Inability to track task progress (x1.4).
27. Human physical capabilities inadequate (x1.4).
28. Lack of job understanding and meaning (x1.4).
29. Emotional stress (x1.3).
30. Ill health (x1.2).
31. Low morale (x1.2).
32. Inconsistency of displays (x1.2).
33. Poor work or immediate task environment (x1.15).
34. Performing boring tasks (x1.1).
35. Sleep cycle disruption (x1.1).
36. Incompatible task pacing (x1.06).
37. Unnecessary staff gatherings (x1.03).
38. Age of personnel (x1.02).

Note how many of the error-producing conditions identified in the HEART methodology refer to initially detecting a sensory input (e.g., #3, a low signal-to-noise ratio). Remember, if something cannot be initially detected or sensed, then it cannot be transmitted to the brain for subsequent processing, decision making, and action selection. In my nuclear power plant incident example, if the control room crew had known (sensed) that one valve was not completely closed prior to issuing the command to open the second valve, then it is highly unlikely that they would have issued this second incorrect order in the first place. In this example, poor visual displays were the culprit (e.g., the displays did not show actual valve status).

Further using my nuclear power plant incident as an example, one can tally the number of error-producing conditions identified in a HEART analysis. Even a short tally includes:

- Very strong negative effect:
  - Unfamiliarity with a situation that is potentially important, but which only occurs infrequently or which is novel.
  - A shortage of time available for error detection and correction (regarding catching the still opened valve).
- Strong to moderate/low negative effect:
  - No means of conveying spatial and functional information to operators, which they can readily assimilate (e.g., bad displays prevented them from being able to determine if the valve was completely closed or still partially opened).
  - No obvious means of reversing an unintended action (once the "open valve" command had been issued, it could not be reversed in a timely manner. Moderate to lower negative effect.
  - Poor, ambiguous, or ill-matched system feedback.
  - No clear direct and timely confirmation of an intended action from the portion of the system over which control is exerted.
  - Operator inexperience.
  - High-level emotional stress.
  - Disruption of normal work–sleep cycles (causing worker fatigue).

Given these numerous, identified, error-producing conditions via HEART, I think it is fairly obvious why the described event occurred. Control room personnel were, unfortunately, set up to fail from the beginning. That is, they were facing an almost insurmountable number of error-producing conditions that simply could not be overcome.

Based on past accident investigations, one observation that I have made is that many work systems are fairly well designed *initially* (or at the very beginning). However, over time, they often begin to slowly and almost imperceptibly degrade; to add, if you will, more and more error-producing conditions and other types of latent factors. This slow degradation process, often called a *drift into failure* in the literature, commonly results in a system migrating almost imperceptibly from a solid and initial "green" condition to a potentially dangerous "yellow" condition, before sometimes experiencing a catastrophic "red" one. These degrading green, yellow, and red conditions can be captured under the following three system states:

1. A *stable, safe, and successfully operating system state* with adequate buffering capacity. A buffer represents the set of mechanical and administrative controls, barriers, etc., that prevents unwanted system-state changes. Although a normal amount of variability certainly exists in this stable state, the system has sufficient buffering capacity to safely accommodate such variances. "Green" indicators of performance truly represent green conditions.

2. An *unstable and unsafe, yet successfully operating, system state* that is approaching a potential critical threshold. A threshold represents the point at which there is an abrupt change in some system quality, property, or state. Prior to actually reaching a critical threshold, gradual changes in underlying driver sets (e.g., introduction of error-producing conditions) usually have little or no apparent impact on system operability, and consequently, a system appears to be operating normally and successfully. A small and often random perturbation (e.g., active or human error) in this threshold zone, however, can initiate a major collapse in system-wide functioning. Small incremental changes, therefore, can eventually have big, often catastrophic effects once a critical threshold is reached. Unlike the previously described stable system state, an indication of "green" here may actually represent a very precarious and potentially dangerous "yellow" condition situation.

3. A *failed system state* with an associated unwanted consequence. A consequence is the degree of resultant harm caused by the adverse system state change as represented by some order of magnitude of loss, disruption, or damage. Unfortunately in this system configuration, red really does mean red.

Note how under the above heading of "unstable and unsafe, yet successfully operating, system state" that the robustness of the system has fundamentally changed from the previous described green state to a new yellow state. Further, in this new yellow state condition, more and more error-producing conditions and other types of latent factors have been introduced into the system over time. Yet, in many instances, system managers remain ignorant of this fundamental and precarious shift in system condition.

For example and as described in much greater detail in Chapter 7, one person in charge of an operation that experienced a catastrophic accident noted that he firmly believed that he "… had every reason to expect that the safeguards, which were in place, were adequate." As will be described in the case study, those safeguards that were *initially* in place were probably adequate. However, over time, those very same in-place safeguards became degraded as more and more error-producing conditions were introduced into the system, some imperceptibly so. In essence, the system began a slow drift into failure that ultimately resulted in a catastrophic ending—a tragic red system state condition, if you will.

The bad news in this discussion is that we humans are almost always the ones who introduce such negative, error-producing conditions into a system. But, the good news is that just as we may sometimes inadvertently or unthinkingly introduce them, we also can remove them, or even better, prevent their introduction from occurring in the first place. Accordingly, the challenge is not in identifying error-producing conditions after an unwanted event occurs (usually during some type of incident investigation). That is the easy part. Rather, the real challenge and admittedly harder part is proactively identifying error-producing conditions before they can combine in an unwanted and oftentimes catastrophic event, or to use tools, such as HEART, to routinely purge a work system of potentially dangerous error-producing conditions, thus keeping green, green.

In summary, sometimes under the right conditions, simple mistakes (or human errors) and systemic organizational weaknesses (called latent factors or error-producing conditions) can combine with deadly consequences. If we are to create safe, reliable, high-quality work systems, then we must do everything possible to minimize the occurrence of human errors. However, we also must recognize that the complete elimination of human error is unrealistic—an essentially human improbability. Accepting this human error reality, we must continuously monitor, identify, and remove potential error-producing conditions from the work setting, thereby significantly reducing the probability of an unwanted incident and, thus, making a system more error tolerant.

I believe the key to this continuous, context-monitoring goal is adopting a so-called "new view" of human error and human performance in general. And, that view, as stated earlier, entails continuously focusing on work setting context; starting during initial design *and* continuously thereafter. We must, therefore, stay forever vigilant in the detection and removal of potential adverse error-producing conditions and other potentially harmful latent factors. For as described, there is no "up side" for the presence of such conditions and factors.

ANALYZING AND IMPROVING HUMAN-RELATED WORK PRODUCTIVITY

Every piece of work in the shops moves. Save 10 steps a day for each of the 12,000 employees, and you will have saved 50 miles of wasted motion and misspent energy.

—Henry Ford

Chapter 5

Human Motion Analysis

As described in Chapter 1, organizations have dual goals. One goal, as previously illustrated in Figure 1.2, is to enhance "success space." Such enhancement efforts often include a healthy dose of improving the efficiency and productivity of various work processes. Another parallel goal is effectively managing "failure space." Here, the challenge is to prevent, or at least significantly negate, the adverse effects or consequences of an unwanted incident.

Many human performance specialists focus almost solely on failure space, especially in studying and investigating the role that human error plays in failure. This preoccupation with failure space and human error is often captured in the titles of many related books and articles, including Dekker's (2006) excellent book, *The Field Guide to Understanding Human Error.*

Yet, I believe that an equally important role for the human performance specialist, one that unfortunately is sometimes overlooked, is in enhancing success space. This observation is particularly relevant for improving human-related work productivity. Frank Gilbreth (see Chapter 1) certainly believed that this was an especially important role, as did Henry Ford. So did Thomas Gilbert.

Thomas Gilbert (1927–1995) is sometimes referred to as the "father" of performance improvement, especially as the founder of what is termed human performance technology or HPT. His book, *Human Competence: Engineering Worthy Performance*, was originally published in 1978. It remains a classic in the field of human performance and is still a valuable and worthwhile read today (thankfully, the book was republished in 1996 by the International Society for Performance Improvement). During his illustrious career, Gilbert served on the faculties of several universities, including Harvard University and the University of Georgia.

In the latter 1980s, I had the honor and privilege of personally meeting Gilbert at a conference in which he spoke. I believe that this was one of the last formal conference presentations that he gave.

One morning during the conference, which was held in San Antonio, Texas, I came down to the lobby in the early morning to fetch a cup of coffee. As I entered the lobby area, I noticed him sitting on a sofa staring intently out the front doors of the hotel. I went over to introduce myself and he immediately told me to be quiet and sit down next to him. I followed his instructions precisely. After all, this was "the" Dr. Gilbert and, at the time, I was just a lowly graduate student working on my doctorate degree.

He was obviously observing the attendants in the valet parking area. I could not tell if he was studying the parking process or simply gawking at the female parking attendants, all of whom were wearing extremely short skirts in the warm morning Texas sunshine. In his defense, he did seem to be taking copious notes. Finally, after about five minutes of sitting quietly and observing, he turned to me and simply said, "Lots of wasted motion."

After those initial words, we chatted a bit. I quickly learned that Dr. Gilbert was a true scholar and gentleman of the old school. He was absolutely delightful to talk with. Now, whenever I think of Thomas Gilbert, I think of that brief meeting and his first "lots of wasted motion" words.

I believe that Gilbreth and Gilbert got it right. That is, if we are to think about improving human work productivity, then we must focus at least some of our efforts on analyzing and identifying, and then eliminating time-consuming and wasted human motions and associated individual task steps. Such wasted motions and steps were what Gilbert was identifying that Texas morning, and what Gilbreth continuously sought to eliminate in the workplace so many years earlier.

By eliminating or at least significantly reducing wasted motions, task-related cycle times also can be significantly reduced. *Cycle time* is defined as the amount of time required to move from one defined point in a process or task to another defined point (Harbour, 1996). Gilbreth, for example, cut some 46 seconds off the average time to lay a single brick by eliminating a number of nonvalue-adding human motions. As a result of eliminating these unneeded actions, his bricklayers could lay a single brick in some 11 seconds, as opposed to the then average time of 57 seconds.

Reducing cycle time (as a consequence of eliminating wasted human motions), in turn, can enable humans to perform more work in the same amount of time (as illustrated by Gilbreth's bricklayers) or perform the same amount of work in much less time. For example, in a hospital emergency room setting, being able to accomplish the same amount of work in much less time is often of critical importance in successfully treating patients suffering life-threatening injuries. A generic illustration of these before-and-after cycle time reduction benefits is depicted in Figure 5.1.

By reducing cycle time, we can likewise improve productivity *and* cut costs simultaneously. George Stalk (1987) attempted to quantify this cycle time–productivity–cost relationship with his developed Rules of Response. His third, ¼ – 2 – 20 rule is of particular relevance here. The rule states that for every quartering or 25 percent reduction in the time interval required to provide a service or product (i.e., meaning cycle time), the productivity of labor and working capital often doubles (the 2 part of his rule). These productivity gains, in turn, can result in as much as a 20 percent reduction in operating costs. By focusing on speed, increases in productivity and decreases in cost can be achieved simultaneously (what is not to like?).

I have been involved in many cycle time reduction efforts over my career and, amazingly, Stalk's calculated ratios invariably hold true. Whenever we have reduced cycle time by some 25 percent, there has always been a roughly parallel 20 percent in accrued cost savings as well.

Based on the importance of eliminating wasted human motions in the work setting, my focus in this chapter is on describing two differing motion analysis techniques. Chapter 6, in turn, centers on discussing some specific ways for improving human productivity, including eliminating previously identified wasted motions.

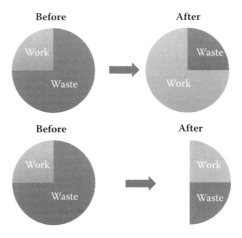

Figure 5.1   Work-related benefits of reducing cycle times.

However, before I attempt to analyze a particular task sequence in order to identify wasted human motions, I normally like to gain some general understanding of the actual task or task sequence itself. In essence, I like to perform a particular type of task analysis that I have found to be quite useful. My goal in this initial task analysis effort is to try and answer the question: "What does someone have to do (and how do they generally have to do it) to achieve a specific and successful task performance outcome?" It is this initial task analysis question that is discussed next.

Task Analysis

Author Robert Fulghum (2004) wrote a fun book titled, *All I Really Need to Know I Learned in Kindergarten.* If I were to ever write a similar book, it would probably be titled, *All I Really Need to Know about Lean Human Performance Improvement I Learned from Baseball.* Although only half joking, I have found baseball, especially baseball in the major leagues, to offer a number of great examples and insights regarding the vagaries of human performance. Therefore, to explain my task analysis approach, I will return once again to Major League Baseball.

In Chapter 3, I described what is actually involved in hitting a 92-mph fastball pitch. For this task analysis-related example, I will move to the infield and focus on the shortstop position (think of Derek Jeter of the New York Yankees). Specifically, I will describe how to conduct a human performance-related task analysis involving fielding a hard hit ground ball to the shortstop position.

Your first reaction might be that this task analysis is incredibly simple. All the shortstop has to do is catch the ball and throw it to the first baseman before the runner arrives, thus getting an out. Admittedly, this is one way to conduct the analysis. However, it does not really provide you with much detailed information. I suggest performing this supposedly simple task analysis in a somewhat different manner.

Remember in the previous chapter (4) I submitted that completing many tasks (e.g., maintenance, surgery, etc.) involves performing:

- *Actions* on
- *Objects* at specified
- *Locations* using various
- *Resources* to some required or inferred
- *Condition* or *specification*.

One can use these five-related components to perform a task analysis as well. An "action" often involves executing a human motion—literally moving some part of the body. For example, turning a valve, connecting a wire, using forceps to plug off a bleeding artery, or carrying a pipe, all represent human actions or motions.

Performed actions also frequently involve objects and resources. Actions also take place at various locations. Finally, to be successful, most actions must meet some predetermined specification. As used here, a specification represents a required performance level or threshold.

Using this action–object–location–resource–specification task framework, I can now begin to analyze a shortstop fielding a hard hit groundball. The *object* is the baseball. Needed *resources* are the gloved hand for catching the ball and the shortstop's other (bare) hand for throwing the ball to first base. There are two identified *locations*. One location is where the ball can be successfully intercepted and caught in the infield after the ground ball is hit. The other location is first base, where the ball must be thrown to gain an out.

To successfully complete this catching and throwing task, there are two required actions: *catching* or fielding the ground ball after it has been hit, and *throwing* the caught ball to the first baseman, all before the base runner reaches the bag.

To successfully catch the ball requires the following discrete task steps:

1. Searching for the hit ball (a perceptual vision task).
2. Detecting (finding) the ball after it has been hit and keeping the ball visually "found" (both perceptual vision tasks).
3. Tracking the ball's progression (a continuing perceptual vision task) while at the same time, immediately moving to a position (a whole body action using the legs) to intercept and catch the ball with a gloved hand (a resource). Physically catching the ball requires "grasping" the ball in the mitt and not dropping the ball after it has been caught.

The next "throwing" portion of the task involves:

4. Moving the bare hand to the glove and grasping and holding the ball.
5. Identifying the location of the first baseman.
6. Throwing the ball to the first baseman.

A success criterion involves making an out. This is, in turn, a function of accuracy and speed. Accuracy requires:

■ Positioning the body and glove in the exact required location to intercept and catch the ball after it has been hit.
■ Throwing the ball to the first baseman in a "catchable" manner—within a specific reachable distance of the first baseman.

Calculating required task speed or time is a bit more difficult. To begin with, I can use differing run times for hitters as they make their way to first base. These run-time figures "bound" required shortstop task times, because the catch and throw to first base must always be just a bit less than hitter run times. As illustrated in Figure 5.2, first base run times vary slightly for left- and right-handed batters, and for above average to below average base runners. The reason for the slight difference in speed between left- and right-handed batters is that a right-handed batter has a few more steps to run to first base than does a left-handed batter. All things being equal, a left-handed batter will beat a right-handed batter to first base every time.

As depicted in Figure 5.2, the shortstop has slightly less than 4.1 to 4.5 seconds to complete the catch and throw task. This slightly less than 4.1 to 4.5 seconds provides a set of defined performance boundaries for the catching and throwing task.

Figure 5.3 graphically depicts a Major League Baseball infield. Figure 5.4 plots a generic hit to the shortstop. In this generic scenario, I am assuming that the ball is hit 125 feet before the shortstop must intersect and catch it. Based on this 125-foot hit distance, a throw distance of approximately 114 feet to the first baseman is required.

Given these catch and throw distances, the next step is to calculate how long it takes the hit ball to reach the shortstop *and* the length of time for the ball to travel to the first baseman after the throw is made to first base. These two calculations require knowing the speed of both the hit ball and the throw

Category	Right-handed Hitter	Left-handed Hitter
Above Average	4.2	4.1
Average	4.3	4.2
Below Average	4.4	4.3
Very Below Average	4.5	4.4

Figure 5.2 First base run times.

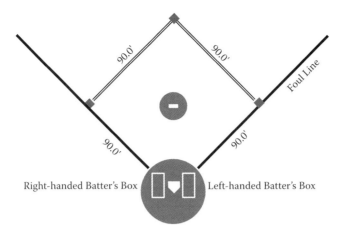

Figure 5.3   Baseball infield dimensions.

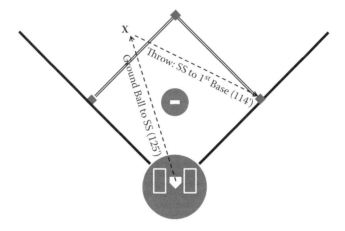

Figure 5.4   Distance of hit ball to shortstop and throw to first base.

to first base. Let us assume that the hit ball travels at 87 mph (a reasonable guess) and the speed of the throw is 80 mph (another reasonable guess).

Based on these figures, we can make the following calculations:

- Ground ball to SS:
  - Distance = 125 ft
  - Speed = 87 mph
  - Time = .98 seconds
- Throw from SS to first base
  - Distance = 114 ft
  - Speed = 80 mph
  - Time = .97 seconds

These calculated hit and throw times are shown in Figure 5.5. Total ball "travel time" involving the hit and the throw is equal to 1.95 seconds (.98 + .97). This combined "ball travel time" figure means that the shortstop has slightly less than 2.15 to 2.55 seconds to transition from catching the ball to throwing the ball to the first baseman. These varying catch-to-throw transition times reflect differing run times to first base, as recorded in Figure 5.2.

For example and as illustrated in Figure 5.6, if the shortstop makes this transitioning action from catch to throw in 2.20 seconds, and total ball travel

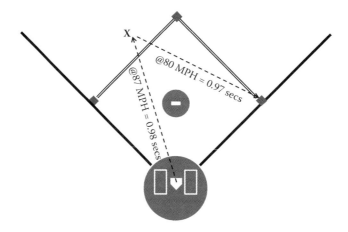

Figure 5.5 Calculated hit and throw times.

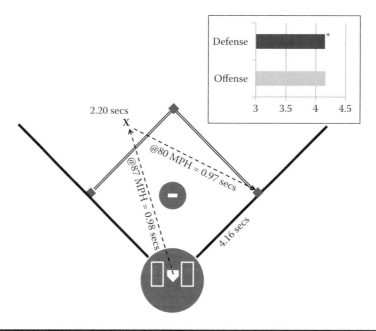

Figure 5.6 Calculated hit and run scenario.

time is 1.95 seconds, then he will complete the catch and throw task in 4.15 seconds. If the batter hitting the ball (who is right-handed) runs to first base in 4.16 seconds, then he will be out by a mere 0.01 seconds. This is the main reason why many outs at first base are so close. Time differences between the base runner and the arriving ball at first base are routinely measured in fractions of a second.

Now let us assume that instead of hitting the ball at 87 mph to the shortstop (but at the same 125-ft distance), the ball travels at a slower 80 mph speed (which, as you will see from the batter's perspective, is a good thing). This slower speed takes 1.07 seconds for the ball to reach the shortstop. If I use the same throw time of .97 seconds, then total baseball travel time is now 0.97 seconds plus 1.07 seconds, for a total time of 2.04 seconds. If catch-to-throw transition time stays at 2.20 seconds, then total task time is 4.24 seconds. If a left-handed batter makes it to first base in a base run time of 4.20 seconds, then he will be safe by a mere 0.04 of a second, as diagrammed in Figure 5.7.

As a historical side note, one of the reasons why Mickey Mantle was such a great baseball player was the fact that he was so speedy in running to first base after hitting the ball. He had one reported first base run time of 3.1 seconds. This fast run time meant that a shortstop would only have about one second, or approximately half the normal time to make

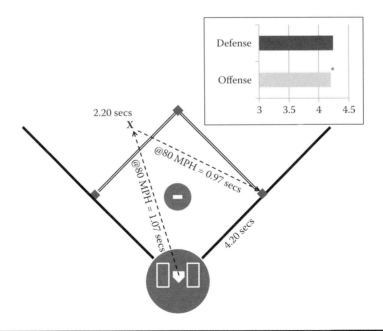

Figure 5.7   Recalculated hit and run scenario.

a catch-to-throw transition. Indeed the success of many of Mantle's single base hits was probably due as much to his speedy base running as it was to his hitting prowess.

Notice how this *action–object–location–resource–specification* task analysis adds a much deeper understanding to what appears to be a rather simple task—catching and throwing a baseball. Using this same, relatively simple technique can provide a similar deeper understanding of critical tasks in the workplace as well. Yet, in many instances, when it comes to analyzing and improving a work task, we sometimes fail to even think about the "what does someone have to actually do (and how do they have to do it) to achieve a specific and successful task outcome" question. As illustrated by my baseball example, systematically answering this question can provide a greater level of task understanding, especially in identifying required human performance levels.

Armed with this initial, more detailed task understanding, my next step is to analyze the real task being performed in much greater detail by physically observing people performing the task. Here, I attempt to answer the question: What is someone currently doing to perform a task and how can that current performance level possibly be improved? Answering this second question almost always involves some type of motion analysis as described next.

Motion Analysis

A *motion analysis* represents a type of performance analysis that focuses on the actions or movements of humans (mostly the hands and feet). In conducting a motion analysis, I normally use two differing analytical techniques:

- Process task analysis (which primarily focuses on gross motor movements, like walking)
- Hand micromotion (therblig) analysis

Think of a zoom lens on a camera. A process task analysis represents a more wide-angle or higher-level motion view. In comparison, a micromotion hand analysis provides a close-up, extreme narrow-angle view (thus providing much greater detail). I also sometimes use what I term a *basic task element analysis,* which falls somewhere between these two views. For a more in-depth description of a process task and basic task element analysis, the reader is referred to my earlier book, titled *The Performance Mapping and Measurement Handbook* (Harbour, 2013c).

Process Task Analysis

A *process task analysis* is a type of process step analysis that focuses on human activities or what the human is doing (or not doing) while performing a task. Note that the same type of analysis also can be used to analyze the actions of a machine, such as an industrial robot.

A process task analysis analyzes a task at the discrete step level. Remember the discussion in Chapter 3 of a discrete and serial skill? A discrete skill represents a skill or task that is organized in such a way that the action is usually brief and has a well-defined beginning and end. Discrete skills often make up serial skills. A serial skill is a type of skill organization that is characterized by several discrete actions linked together in a temporal sequence, often with the order of the actions being crucial to performance success.

In conducting a process task analysis, the goal is to identify all discrete actions (and inactions) in their proper order that comprises a serial-type task. Time measurements for each discrete task step are further collected and recorded.

A process task analysis uses five differing generic task step types and associated symbols, as summarized in Figure 5.8. The five generic steps include:

- *Operation*: Any value-adding step directly moving a task forward (a circle).
- *Transportation*: Any step that moves (transports) something, including a human walking (an arrow).

Step	Step Symbol	Description
Operation	●	Any value-adding step directly moving a process forward.
Transportation	➡	Any step that moves (i.e., transports) something (includes a human walking).
Inspection	■	Quality inspections, authorizations, and reviews.
Delay	▷	Unscheduled delay of parts, people, materials, and products.
Rework	Ⓡ	Any steps unnecessarily repeated step, especially repeated operation steps.

Figure 5.8   Generic process task analysis step types.

- *Inspection*: Determining the quality or specification of something (a square).
- *Delay*: Unscheduled human "waiting" time (a stretched out "D").
- *Rework*: Unnecessarily repeating a previous step (often due to a defect), especially a previous operation step (a circle with an "R" in the middle).

Note that each step type also can be thought of as a higher-level human action or motion. In regards to the task step "delay," it represents an inaction or "nonmotion." In some process analysis methods, a sixth type of task step termed *storage* is added. Storage refers to scheduled delays of parts, materials, and products, such as occurs when warehousing an item. Humans, however, cannot be stored. They can only be delayed.

When conducting a process task analysis, one simply observes a human performing a particular task and records discrete task steps in their sequential order. Ensuing time intervals for all individual steps are collected and recorded as well. A process task analysis worksheet is used to record all task-related discrete step types, step sequences, and associated step times (as illustrated in Figure 5.9).

To begin practicing how to conduct a human performance-related process task analysis, I suggest that you first analyze some differing tasks at home. Pick a task and perform it in a couple of different ways. Then analyze those two different ways via a process task analysis. Once you become comfortable using the methodology at home, then you can then try it at work.

Step #	Step Description	Flow	Time (Secs)	Notes
1	Walk to kitchen (empty handed).	➡	11.2	
2	Grasp and remove coffee pot from coffeemaker.	●	2.1	
3	Carry coffee pot back to living room.	➡	9.9	
4	Pour coffee into coffee cup.	●	4.6	
5	Carry coffee pot back to kitchen.	➡	10.3	
6	Place coffee pot in coffeemaker.	●	1.8	
7	Walk back to chair in living room and be seated.	➡	10.7	
		Total	50.6	

Figure 5.9 "Coffee pot to coffee cup" process task analysis worksheet.

For example, each morning my wife and I have coffee together. In the winter, we sit in front of the fireplace in our living room for our coffee-drinking ritual. In the summertime, we move out to the front porch. We each drink exactly two cups of coffee. Because I normally get up before she does, I am usually drinking my second cup of coffee while she is still drinking her first cup. When she is finished drinking her first cup, I almost always get up to get her a refill.

I perform this "refill coffee cup" task in one of two ways. One way is to take the empty coffee cup out to the kitchen and pour the second cup there. The other way is that I walk to the kitchen first, grab the coffee pot out of the coffee maker, and return it to the living room where I then pour the second cup. Which task sequence is more efficient?

To conduct my coffee cup-pouring analysis, I conduct two different process task analyses, one for each cup-pouring technique. For each analysis, I record involved steps in their proper sequence and all associated times on a process task analysis worksheet.

Figure 5.9 is the process task analysis worksheet for bringing the "coffee pot to the coffee cup" in the living room. Figure 5.10 records the task sequence for bringing the "coffee cup to the coffee pot" in the kitchen. I next summarize my results in a comparison table (sometimes called a before–after improvement chart), as illustrated in Figure 5.11.

Step #	Step Description	Flow	Time (Secs)	Notes
1	Get up from chair and walk to wife's chair.	→	1.9	
2	Grasp and remove coffee cup.	●	1.4	
3	Carry empty coffee cup to coffeemaker in kitchen.	→	10.4	
4	Remove coffee pot and pour coffee into cup.	●	6.8	
5	Replace coffee pot in coffeemaker.	●	3.6	
6	Carry full coffee cup to wife in living room and place coffee cup on coffee table.	→	10.7	
7	Return to and be seated in chair.	→	1.9	
		Total	36.7	

Figure 5.10   "Coffee cup to coffee pot" process task analysis worksheet.

	Coffee Pot to Coffee Cup		Coffee Cup to Coffee Pot	
Step Type	**# of Steps**	**Time (Secs)**	**#of Steps**	**Time (Secs)**
Operation	3	8.5	3	11.8
Transportation	4	42.1	4	24.9
Delay				
Inspection				
Rework				
Total	**7**	**50.6**	**7**	**36.7**

Figure 5.11   Comparative "coffee pouring" analysis summary table.

Based on the described coffee cup analysis, I can now quantitatively and objectively make the following observations:

■ From my perspective (the worker), it takes seven different steps totaling 50.6 seconds to bring the coffee pot to the coffee cup. In comparison, although it also takes seven individual task steps to take the coffee cup to the coffee pot, total elapsed task time is only 36.7 seconds, a savings of 13.9 seconds. The identified savings in time for this second task sequence are the result of eliminating two kitchen back-and-forth transportation steps, which are the longest step times in the "coffee pot to coffee cup" sequence. As recorded in the summary table in Figure 5.11, cumulative transportation step time for the "coffee pot to coffee cup" task sequence is 42.1 seconds. However, for the "coffee cup to coffee pot" sequence, total transportation step time is reduced to 24.9 seconds. Note also in this second task sequence, I am physically walking less, as measured by total transportation distance.

■ If I did nothing but poured my wife cups of coffee for a solid hour, using the "coffee pot to coffee cup" task sequence, I could pour some 71 cups of coffee. But, by using the shorter "coffee cup to coffee pot" task sequence, I would pour approximately 98 cups in the same hour, a productivity increase of 27 poured cups of coffee or some 38 percent. By focusing on saving mere seconds per task step, I have translated those microsavings into a much larger productivity gain at the hour or day level, essentially the same thing that Frank Gilbreth did in laying more bricks.

■ From my wife's perspective, however, who is the *customer* in this scenario, things appear slightly differently. In the "coffee pot to coffee cup" task sequence, she gets her second cup of coffee in 27.8 seconds. However, in the "coffee cup to coffee pot" sequence, her second cup of coffee does not arrive for 34.8 seconds, some seven seconds later.

Obviously these differences in mere seconds are insignificant to my wife. But, in some work settings, such minor differences can be very important. For example, imagine that an emergency room (ER) nurse must perform a time-critical task on a patient with just minutes to live. In this case, the fastest time from the patient's perspective is the most important one (the "coffee pot to coffee cup" task sequence). However, if that same nurse has to perform two critical tasks in succession, she would get an almost 14-second jump start on performing the second task if she followed the "coffee cup to coffee pot" sequence.

Thinking about task design in this way can help us make more intelligent decisions about the best way to perform both a single task and a series of separate, but sequential tasks. And, this type of task-related thinking must always include a healthy appreciation for analyzing, identifying, and eliminating time-consuming wasted human motions.

The important point here is obviously not about how to pour coffee in the speediest manner possible, but rather how to systematically go about collecting quantitative task-related data, and then using that gathered data to make objective, fact-based decisions; especially decisions involving where and how to improve a task sequence. As illustrated in my coffee cup example, often very minor savings in time can translate into huge savings, especially for highly repetitive task sequences. Such time savings can translate, in turn, into significant increases in productivity and reductions in operating costs.

Before leaving this discussion on how to conduct a process task analysis, a few helpful hints are offered:

■ If the task of interest is going to be performed only once, then I strongly suggest that you videorecord it. The same goes if task action is fast-paced. Studies have shown that humans can miss as much as 70 percent of the action in a fast-paced sports setting. Imagine, for example, that you are trying to analyze the individual motions of pit crew members changing tires during a NASCAR race. All of that pit crew action is over in less than 15 seconds. In such instances, videorecording is an absolute necessity.

■ If you are analyzing a task that is repeated over and over again, take enough measures to properly "time-bound" the task. Additionally, be very sensitive to how different people perform the exact same task. I once watched two nurses in the same ER unit perform an identical task. Yet, it seemed that the one nurse took three to four times longer to complete the task than did the other nurse. The question is why? As illustrated by the ER example, there is often one best way to perform a task. The challenge is always to find that best way.

■ If the same task sequence is being repeated over and over, I first watch that sequence once or twice to gain a better familiarity of the individually involved (and discrete) task steps. Next, I fill in all identified task steps in their proper sequence on a preformatted worksheet that I bring with me (see Figure 5.12). Finally, I record a number of time measures while observing different iterations of the same task, all the time still using my preformatted process task analysis worksheet.

■ In timing individual discrete task steps, I often use the "stopwatch" function on the "Clock" application on my Apple iPad (the iPhone has the same app). At the beginning of the task sequence I tap "Start." At the completion of each individual discrete step, I hit the "Lap" button. Just remember to hit the "Stop" button on the last lap or step. Lap times are displayed in reverse order on the screen (e.g., 5, 4, 3, 2, and 1). So make sure that you correlate the right task step number and time with the right lap number and time (do not reverse them).

Observed Task:		Date:		Time of Day:		
Location:		Analyst:				
Step #	Step Description	Step Times #1	Step Times #2	Step Times #3	Step Times #4	

Figure 5.12   Blank process task analysis worksheet.

▪ You may want to label the individual step types (e.g., operation, transportation, etc.) in greater detail. In my coffee cup illustration, I would probably label the transport steps as "transport empty," meaning not carrying anything, and "transport loaded." This greater step detail is essentially what a basic task element analysis consists of (see Harbour, 2013c, for a fuller explanation).

The reader may be wondering how a generic task analysis as described in the previous section ties into a more specific and observable process task analysis as presented here. Consider once again the shortstop baseball example. If my actual observation-based process task analysis reveals that a shortstop is routinely taking 2.6 to 2.9 seconds to transition from catching the ball to throwing the ball, I immediately know where at least one problem lies (he is too slow in this catch-to-throw transition task step motion). This identified problem area now becomes an immediate potential improvement area.

By better understanding required task performance levels (especially at the discrete task step level), I can compare what I expect to find versus what I actually observe and find. Such expected versus observed comparisons add a great deal to a process task analysis, often making performance problem and subsequent improvement area identification much easier. This observation is particularly true when the unit of measurement is often mere seconds, and even fractions of seconds.

Though much can be learned from a higher-level process task analysis, a more detailed, close-up view is sometimes needed to truly understand and analyze a task sequence. This comment is especially true in analyzing more complex "operation" steps. Additionally, many complex operation steps involve using our hands. Not only is the devil in the details when it comes to analyzing and improving human work productivity, but it is also often "in the hands." As described next, learning how to analyze hand motions at the microstep level can add a great deal of information to any motion-related task analysis.

Micromotion Hand Analysis

As much as we use our senses, brain, and nervous system in the work setting, most work—the directly observable part—is actually performed using our hands (although our senses, brain, and nervous system are all required to physically "use" our hands). As previously noted, human hands represent extremely versatile tools that are capable of performing tasks ranging from fine precision, such as threading a needle, to great strength, such as swinging a sledgehammer. Indeed in many respects, our success as a species is due in large part to our ability to grasp and manipulate objects with our hands, along with being bipedal or walking upright on two legs, and having a large brain.

As described in Chapter 3, the key to why our hands are so effective and tool-capable is because of our strong opposable thumbs. That opposable thumb makes prehension or grasping possible. Without the thumb, the human hand instantly loses many of its remarkable functions.

Frank Gilbreth developed a strong appreciation for the human hand, understanding that most manual work is performed by way of various hand motions. Additionally, Gilbreth learned early in his career that carefully observing the hand motions of his workers could tell him a great deal about the efficiency of the work being performed. He further recognized that manual hand work consists of a relatively few fundamental motions that are performed over and over again. From a hand perspective, "manually" performing surgery and working on a car involve essentially the same repetitive hand motions (albeit, those same hand motions are using decidedly different tools). Accordingly, the term *manual work* in reference to hand motion analysis refers to any work activity that is hand-intensive, irrespective of specific work setting.

Based on this human hand appreciation, Gilbreth developed a hand-centric analytical and improvement method called *therblig analysis*. "Therblig" is Gilbreth spelled backwards except for the beginning "th." Today, some authors use the term "hand micromotion study" when referring to a therblig analysis. A hand micromotion study probably has more descriptive meaning, especially to someone unfamiliar with the therblig concept.

According to Gilbreth, *therbligs* are the basic building blocks of virtually all manual work that is performed at a single location, such as when someone is sitting or standing at a workbench or operating table. Therbligs involve physical motions of the hands. They also involve sensing (involving primarily the eyes) and mentally processing that sensed information with the brain. One can think of therbligs as observable and repetitive "micro outcomes" of the sensing, processing, signaling, and moving cycle described in Chapter 3.

Kato (1991) provides an excellent overview of therblig analysis. His proposed therblig classification system, based on Gilbreth's original work, is essentially adopted here with some minor exceptions. Although Kato identifies 18 different therbligs, I and many others use only 17 therbligs, eliminating the "find" therblig. When the human eye finds something, the hand almost immediately grasps it ("grasp" is also a therblig). I personally find it difficult to differentiate between the therbligs "find" and "grasp." "Grasp" I can physically observe, "find" I cannot.

Additionally, Gilbreth developed a graphical symbol for each therblig, as well as an abbreviation using one or two letters. I find using the abbreviated letters much easier than having to draw out each therblig symbol. Accordingly, I will use only abbreviations when describing therbligs here. If interested in what these various symbols look like, the reader is referred to Kato (1991).

Kato further divides therbligs into three major types of motions, as summarized in Figure 5.13.

■ *Type 1 motions* involve those motions required for performing an operational task. Type 1 motions primarily involve hand motions that pick up, use, process, combine, or otherwise manipulate an object that is essential to an operation. As depicted in Figure 5.13, nine different therbligs are classified as Type 1 motions.

Motion Type	Therblig	Symbol
Type 1 Motions	1. Transport Empty	TE
	2. Grasp	G
	3. Transport Loaded	TL
	4. Release Load	RL
	5. Position	P
	6. Use	U
	7. Disassemble	DA
	8. Assemble	A
	9. Inspect	I
Type 2 Motions	1. Search	Sh
	2. Select	St
	3. Plan	Pn
	4. Pre-Position	PP
Type 3 Motions	1. Hold	H
	2. Unavoidable Delay	UD
	3. Avoidable Delay	AD
	4. Rest	R

Figure 5.13   Therblig motion summary table.

■ *Type 2 motions* tend to slow down Type 1 motions. According to Kato, they involve "… more thinking than doing." Four different therbligs comprise this Type 2 motion category.

■ *Type 3 motions* do not perform an operational task. These types of motions consist of activities that prevent an operation from occurring and result only in task delay. Often they represent some type of "standby" motion in which the human performer simply holds an object for the time being. Four individual therbligs involve Type 3 motions.

In the following subsections, individual therbligs are described under each motion type (Type 1, 2, and 3). Note that the right and left hand may be performing different therbligs and different motion types at the same time. Also, the term *object* as used here refers to any tool, needed material, resource, etc. Think of an object as being essentially anything that can be picked up and held with one or two hands. In the following graphical illustrations, the "object" is the saltshaker being used.

Type 1 Motions

Nine different therbligs comprise Type 1 motions.

1. *Transport empty (TE)*. The transport empty therblig (abbreviated by the capital letters *TE*) indicates a hand that is moving while empty. Think of a crane moving to pick something up. It is moving or "transporting empty." During transport empty, the hand is often moving forward for a specific purpose. In such forward-moving instances, transport empty is normally followed by a *grasp* motion. A "transport empty" hand also can be moving backward after having moved for a specific purpose, such as releasing an object. In this case, the hand is simply moving to a previous position. *TE* begins when the hand begins to move without load or resistance, and ends when the hand stops moving. Note in Figure 5.14 that, in the left-hand photo, the hand is just beginning to move (*TE*) toward the saltshaker. In the right-hand photo, the hand is nearing the end of the *TE* motion as it begins to grasp the saltshaker.

2. *Grasp (G)*. The hand touching an object is what completes the previous transport empty motion. After touching an object, the hand grasps the object. This grasping motion normally involves closing or clasping

Figure 5.14 Beginning (left) and ending (right) transport empty (TE) motion. (Photo courtesy of Chris Harbour.)

Figure 5.15 Ending grasp (*G*) motion. (Photo courtesy of Chris Harbour.)

Figure 5.16 Beginning transport loaded (*TL*) motion. (Photo courtesy of Chris Harbour.)

the fingers around an object. *G* begins when the hand or fingers first makes contact with the object, and ends when the hand has obtained control of it. An ending grasp motion is illustrated in Figure 5.15. Note how this grasp motion occurs between the transport empty motion depicted in Figure 5.14 and the transport loaded motion illustrated in Figure 5.16.

3. *Transport loaded (TL).* The therblig transport loaded (also sometimes called *carry*) basically occurs when a hand that is holding some object moves (or "carries" that object) from one place to another. As described by Kato (1991), *TL* can take many different forms, including the hand:
   - Carrying something through the air
   - Pushing something
   - Sliding something
   - Pulling something
   - Dragging something
   - Rolling something

   TL begins when the grasped object starts to move and ends when the object stops moving. A beginning transport loaded motion immediately following a grasp motion is illustrated in Figure 5.16.

4. *Release load (RL).* The release load therblig is any motion that lets go of an object. Normally release load follows the "transport loaded" motion. *RL* begins when the object starts to leave the hand and ends when the object has been completely separated from the hand or fingers.

5. *Position (P).* The position motion puts or places the object in the correct position for the next motion, moving it while or after it is being carried. "Position" involves turning or locating an object in such a way that it will be properly oriented to fit into the location for which it is intended. It is often possible to position an object during the motion "transport loaded." In such instances, the combined motion should be indicated as *TL + P*. *P* begins when the hand begins to turn or locate the object, and ends when the object has been placed in the desired position or location.

6. *Use (U).* The use motion represents any motion that uses an object (e.g., a tool) for a particular purpose. "Use" commonly involves manipulating a tool, device, or piece of apparatus for the purpose for which it is intended. *U* begins when the hand starts to manipulate the tool or device, and ends when the hand ceases the application. Two views of a use motion are illustrated in Figure 5.17. In the second view, the person is literally shaking the saltshaker, or "using" it for its intended purpose.

7. *Disassemble (DA).* The therblig "disassemble" represents the motion of taking apart something that has been put together, or separating one object from another object for which it is an integral part of. *DA* begins when the hand starts to remove one part from the assembly and ends when the hand has separated the part completely from the remainder of the assembly. Removing a nut from a bolt is an example of the disassemble motion.

Figure 5.17   Two views of the use (*U*) motion. (Photo courtesy of Chris Harbour.)

8. *Assemble (A)*. The assemble motion is any motion that inserts or adds one object into or onto another object, such as threading a nut onto a bolt. It involves placing one object into or on another object with which it becomes an integral part of. Kato (1991) makes an important point regarding the assemble therblig when he notes that assemble motions do not work well "unless they are preceded by a position motion." This position motion immediately prior to an assemble motion is represented as $P > A$ or, more likely, as $TL + P > A$. *A* begins as the hand starts to move the part into its place in the assembly motion and ends when the hand has completed the assembly.

9. *Inspect (I)*. The inspect therblig often involves examining an individual or assembled object in order to determine whether or not that object compiles with some standard size, shape, color, or other previously determined and required quality value. Inspections may employ sight (normally), hearing, touch, odor, or even taste. Accordingly, the inspect "motion" is predominantly a mental reaction and may occur with other therbligs. *I* begins when the eyes or other parts of the human sensory system begin to examine the object and ends when the examination is completed.

Type 2 Motions

There are four Type 2 therblig motions. Remember, Type 2 motions tend to slow down Type 1 motions and involve more thinking than doing.

1. *Search (Sh)*. Search involves the eyes (sometimes other senses as well) and/or hands hunting or groping for an object. *Sh* begins when the eyes and/or hands begin to hunt for an object and ends when the object

has been found. Kato (1991) notes that sometimes the start and stop of a search motion is a fairly subjective determination on the part of the observer. He offers three general guidelines for this motion:

a. It is *not* a search if a person already knows what the object he or she is looking for is and its approximate location.

b. Conversely, it is a search if the person knows what the object he or she is looking for is, but *does not* know its location.

c. The searching motion comes to an end as soon as the object is picked up (Grasp). Also, an object may be hidden from view by something. Search ends when the thing blocking the view of an object is removed.

2. *Select (St).* The select motion usually follows searching for an object and successfully finding a group that contains that object. It indicates actually selecting the object from that group. In actual practice, however, it is oftentimes extremely difficult (if not impossible) to determine where *search* ends and *select* begins. Accordingly, search and select are often combined under the therblig of "select." In this search–select motion combination, select now refers to the hunting and locating of one object from among several objects. At this higher level, *St* begins when the eyes and/or hands begin to hunt for the object and ends when the desired object has been located (usually just immediately prior to "grasp"). Within this broader definition of select, moving an empty hand forward (transport empty) is now incorporated into the "select" motion. However, and as described under "search," if a person knows the approximate location of an object, then moving a hand forward is not part of a search motion. It is a transport empty (*TE*) motion.

3. *Plan (Pn).* Plan represents a mental activity that involves deciding how to proceed with a work task. It normally precedes a physical movement. *Pn* begins at the point where a person begins to work out the next step of a task and ends when that next following step has been determined.

4. *Preposition (PP).* Preposition involves placing an object in a predetermined place. It can also include placing an object in its correct position for some subsequent motion. For example and as described by Kato (1991), placing the handle of a teapot in an upright position so that it is easier for the next person to reach is a "preposition" motion. "Position" and "preposition" motions are similar except that in preposition, an object is placed in the approximate position or configuration that is required for a later motion.

Type 3 Motions

Type 3 motions do not directly perform a task. There are four Type 3 motions.

1. *Hold (H).* The hold motion indicates that the object is just being held and is not being used for anything—no movement of the object is taking place. However, care must be used here. For a right-handed person, the left-hand often holds something while the right-hand is "working" on the object with a Type 1 motion. For example, after inserting a needle to draw blood, a right-handed nurse will often "hold" the syringe with her left hand while drawing blood with her right hand (a "use" motion). In this particular instance, it is advisable to also identify the left-hand "hold" motion as a "use" motion as both hands are operating or "using" the syringe. *H* begins when the movement of the object stops and ends with the next therblig motion.

2. *Unavoidable delay (UD).* An unavoidable delay is a delay caused by something for which the person performing the task is not responsible (e.g., it is beyond that person's control). *UD* may be caused by a failure or interruption in a work process. It begins when the hand stops its activity and ends when the hand resumes the same activity.

3. *Avoidable Delay (AD).* An avoidable delay is a delay or standby motion that can be completely eliminated if the right kind of change or improvement is made in a task sequence. As described by Kato (1991), one of the main points of therblig analysis "… is to find avoidable delays and to make improvements that eliminate them." *AD* begins when a prescribed sequence of motions is interrupted and ends when that sequence is resumed.

4. *Rest (R).* Rest indicates that the person performing a task is resting (perhaps to recover from fatigue) and no work is being performed. In some instances, rest periods are purposely built into a work sequence. In other instances, however, rest periods may be a sign of fatigue, indicating that the work and its required tools are too exhausting. *R* begins when the worker stops working and ends when work is resumed.

Note how the "grasp" motion underlies many other therbligs. For example, we cannot transport, use, position, assemble, disassemble, or hold an object unless we first grasp that object and keep on "grasping" it. This is what makes our hands so unique. Via an opposable thumb, humans can grasp almost anything, either with just a few fingers or the whole hand.

Admittedly, conducting a therblig analysis takes a bit of practice and getting used to. My advice is to start with very simple tasks, especially tasks at home, and build from there. For example, you are at the dinner table and grab the saltshaker to sprinkle a bit of salt on your food. How would these motions look from a therblig analytical point of view?

Let us assume that you know what the object is that you are looking for (the saltshaker) and its approximate location on the kitchen table (e.g., no search or select are required). Also assume that you are right-handed. This right-handed motion sequence would involve:

1. Reaching for the saltshaker (a transport empty or *TE* motion).
2. Grasping the saltshaker (a grasp or *G* motion).
3. Moving the saltshaker back to your plate (a transport loaded or *TL* motion).
4. Sprinkling salt on your food (a use or *U* motion).
5. Returning the saltshaker to its original approximate position on the table (a transport loaded or *TL* motion).
6. Placing the saltshaker back on the table (a release load or *RL* motion).
7. Returning your hand back to its former position by your plate (a transport empty or *TE* motion).

This therblig motion sequence is represented as: *TE* > *G* > *TL* > *U* > *TL* > *RL* > *TE*. Actual photos of someone performing the first four motions of the described task sequence are illustrated in Figures 5.14 (*TE*), 5.15 (*G*), 5.16 (*TL*), and 5.17 (*U*).

Note in this saltshaker example that all motions represent Type 1 motions, indicating that all of these motions are required to perform the saltshaker-using task. One cannot really use or "shake" a saltshaker, for example, if it is not first grasped. Accordingly, no single motion can be eliminated from this described saltshaker therblig sequence (although the various transport motions could be shortened if the saltshaker was located closer to the person).

If the saltshaker, however, is hidden from view behind the ketchup bottle and you have to initially search for it, then this changes my analysis a bit. In this case, the beginning motion is a Type 2 search (*Sh*) motion. Remember, Type 2 motions tend to slow down Type 1 motions. So, in this case, having to initially search for the saltshaker is slower than moving your hand (*TE*) directly toward it.

You might wonder about your left hand during this saltshaker retrieve and use task. If you are holding a knife in your left hand and simply continue to hold it, then the left-hand motion would be hold (*H*), a Type 3 motion. If your left hand is "empty" and simply sitting on the table doing nothing, then this would be recorded as a rest (*R*) or avoidable delay (*AD*) hand motion.

Let us try another example. This time, you want to thread a nut onto a bolt. You hold the bolt in your left hand (a "use" therblig because this motion is required to perform the assembly task) while threading the nut onto it with your right hand. I also will assume that the nut is in a can with other nuts of different sizes. In this case, the right hand must:

1. Select (*St*) the proper nut from the can (by also using the eyes).
2. Grasp (*G*) the correct nut from the can.
3. Move (transport loaded or *TL*) and position (*P*) the nut to the bolt (*TL* + *P*).
4. Thread the nut onto the bolt (assemble or *A*).

This right-handed micromotion task sequence is represented as: $St > G > TL + P > A$.

Note that in this example, unlike the previous saltshaker example, there is a Type 2 motion in the sequence and that is the therblig select (*St*). This "select" therblig motion slows down the execution of the follow-on grasp motion.

When conducting a therblig analysis, I almost always video-record the motion sequence first, unless it is extremely simple like the saltshaker or bolt examples. Reportedly, Frank Gilbreth could easily record all hand motion sequences, even complex ones, in real time. I am simply not that fast and I find most people are not either.

When viewing a hand-motion video, I record each left- or right-hand motion on a blank therblig analysis worksheet, as illustrated in Figure 5.18. If nothing is recorded in the column for either the left or right hand, then that absence implies that the hand is not in use. The "eye" column is primarily reserved for the "search" and "inspect" therbligs. A completed right-hand therblig analysis worksheet for my saltshaker example is depicted in Figure 5.19.

Also note that times are usually not recorded in a therblig analysis, because most hand motions are executed in literally fractions of a second. Instead, the goal of a therblig analysis is somewhat akin to a "hunt and destroy" mission, with the focus on identifying and eliminating as many Type 2 and Type 3 motions as possible, as well as shortening all transport distances.

In summary, a therblig analysis is a micromotion hand analysis. It can provide a great deal of information about a specific operational step,

#	Task Element	Left-hand Motion	Therblig			Right-hand Motion
			Left hand	Eyes	Right Hand	

Figure 5.18   Blank therblig analysis worksheet.

Task Element	#	Left-hand Motion	Therblig			Right-hand Motion
			Left hand	Eyes	Right Hand	
Sprinkle salt on food	1				TE	Reach for salt shaker
	2				G	
	3				TL	
	4				U	Sprinkle salt
	5				TL	
	6				RL	
	7				TE	Return hand to plate

Figure 5.19   Completed saltshaker therblig analysis worksheet example.

especially wasted micromotions within that operational step sequence. As stated above, the important point in performing a therblig analysis is identifying all wasted motions, especially Type 2 and Type 3 motions.

One question that I am frequently asked is when a process task- and/or a therblig-motion analysis should be conducted. A somewhat related question that I sometimes hear is: "Who actually uses this stuff?" Both questions are briefly addressed in the following final section.

Application

One prime candidate for human motion analyses is brief, short-duration, highly repetitive tasks or task sequences. As demonstrated in the above examples, savings of just a few seconds per individual task step can translate into significant gains in productivity and associated reductions in operating costs when aggregated by the hour or day. Additionally, such microsavings result in more work being accomplished for the same or less amount of human exertion (e.g., fatigue). As such, small improvements in these highly repetitive types of tasks can result in big productivity gains.

Unfortunately, many Lean Six Sigma improvement efforts overlook these short duration tasks, thinking they have little to offer. Instead, improvement teams often go after so-called big and costly "hitters." However, I have found just the opposite to be true. In point of fact, some of my biggest productivity gains, working as either an internal or external performance improvement consultant, have come from cutting mere seconds off of highly repetitive task sequences. So, it often pays to think micro small, while accruing macro big.

A second favorable candidate area involves any type of critical time-sensitive task. In these types of tasks, time is of the essence. In manufacturing, for example, setup and turnaround tasks often fall in this time-sensitive category. Although these types of tasks are necessary, they normally disrupt production. As such, keeping setup and turnaround times to an absolute minimum is critical in many production settings.

Another area where human motion analyses can potentially pay huge dividends is in settings where work time is fixed and of a relatively short duration. For example, personnel involved in the massive cleanup effort at the Japanese Fukushima nuclear reactor complex are severely limited as to the amount of time that they can physically work in a radioactively con-taminated area. Often they can only work in these "hot" areas for some 10 to 30 minutes at a time. In these time-limited instances, maximizing the amount of work that can be accomplished is extremely important.

In summary, important candidates for motion analyses, whether at the higher process task analysis level or at the therblig microanalysis level, include short duration, highly repetitive tasks, *and* time-sensitive tasks.

Answering the "who actually uses this stuff" question is a bit more difficult. Perhaps the truthful answer is not as many people as could or should. I think one reason for this paucity of use is that many improvement specialists simply lack the requisite skills and corresponding practice in applying human motion analysis. Yet, hopefully, as demonstrated in the previous sections, these techniques are quite easy to master and can be extremely powerful. Additionally, successfully learning how to analyze pouring coffee or using a saltshaker is really no different than analyzing more complex tasks in the workplace. At the individual discrete task step level, human hand and foot motions are basically all the same. So, start simple and build from there.

Interestingly, there is one group of folks who seem to be almost natural motion analysts and improvement specialists, although they probably do not think of themselves in this regard. Consider for example, just three of their "Lean" exploits:

■ Shortly after 3 a.m. on October 16, 2012, two men entered the Kunsthal Museum in Rotterdam, The Netherlands. Ninety-six seconds later, they were recorded on security video cameras exiting the museum. Alarms sounded only as the two thieves left the museum. In those short 96 seconds while inside the museum, the thieves stole seven paintings, including Monet's *Waterloo Bridge, London*, Gauguin's *Girl in Front of Open Window*, and Picasso's *Harlequin Head*. The value of the stolen paintings exceeded $100 million.

■ On February 19, 2013, eight heavily armed men, driving two black vehicles with police markings and flashing lights, breached a security fence at Brussels International Airport in Belgium. The two vehicles drove straight to a Swiss Helvetic Airways passenger jet preparing to pull back from a departure gate. The plane, carrying uncut diamonds in its still-opened rear cargo hold, was bound for Zurich, Switzerland. The armed thieves made off with 120 parcels of diamonds valued at some $50 million. The complete in-fence time for the diamond heist was 11 minutes. The actual theft at the plane took less than three minutes.

■ On the night of February 12, 1994, a man climbed a ladder to the second floor of the National Gallery in Oslo, Norway. Some 50 seconds later (as recorded on security video cameras), the thief dropped the painting *The Scream* by Edmund Munch to a waiting accomplice on the ground. At the time of the theft, the painting was valued at $72 million. After later being recovered, it sold at auction for $199.9 million.

In each of these thefts, speed was the key; the bad guys were faster than the responding good guys. As described by author Edward Dolnick (2005) regarding the theft of *The Scream*, "… if the thieves could get in and out quickly enough, the best alarms would provide little more than background noise."

As I have studied these super-fast grab and go art and diamond heists, what has perhaps impressed me the most is the incredible amount of upfront analysis and planning (and probably lots of associated practice) that precedes each heist. Indeed, great heists seem to require exquisite timing, and that "exquisite timing" is achieved through incredible planning. Selby and Campbell (2012) capture this upfront commitment to detailed planning when they note that "… at the heart of every successful heist was a near-religious devotion to research." The authors further describe one preheist planning session this way: "The room was filled with notebooks, sketches, and maps, the material they needed to run through each part of the operation, to visualize every element of the break-in and make sure nothing was overlooked."

I am certainly not advocating that we all quit our day jobs and take our Lean improvement skills to the darker side of the law. However, I do think that we can learn something from studying these heists, and that is, upfront task analysis and planning can enable some incredible, time-based accomplishments. Perhaps then, we should attempt to duplicate this attention to detail in our own workplace settings. This increased understanding would certainly include realizing the importance of identifying and eliminating time-consuming and wasted human motions and associated task steps, thereby allowing us to "get in and out quickly enough."

Chapter 6

Human Productivity Improvement

In the previous chapter, I described two motion analysis techniques. One technique, called *process task analysis*, focuses primarily on gross motor movements. The second technique, termed *hand micromotion* or *therblig analysis*, is chiefly focused on hand movements. However, if you have a hard time remembering all of this motion-related verbiage, then a bare-bones shortcut is to just remember feet and hands.

Our feet enable gross locomotion or transport. Foot locomotion also requires leg locomotion. Feet-related transport may involve moving empty handed, which is often termed *transport empty*. Human transport also can entail carrying something in one or both hands. This type of transport is often referred to as *transport loaded*.

Similarly, our hands also produce a number of motions, mostly at the fine motor movement level. Like our feet requiring our legs, hands require our arms. Arm length often limits selected hand motion "reach" as described later.

Improving human-related motion performance, which, in turn, directly increases human work productivity, can take many differing forms. Yet, over many years of being involved in various performance improvement efforts, I have found that some basic human motion improvement strategies— themes, if you wish—are used over and over again. That is, whereas the how and where of human motion improvement seems to vary widely, the basic underlying strategies that support the "how" and "where" stay fairly consistent. I have identified six such reoccurring strategies and have come to call them my Universal Motion Improvement Strategies list.

#	Strategy	Major Body Part(s)	Principle Improvement Area(s)
1	Minimize the number of feet-related transport empty motions.	Feet	Redesign task
2	Shorten all transport "walking" routes as much as possible.	Feet	Redesign layout
3	Avoid all avoidable delays.	Feet and hands	Redesign task and/or layout
4	Eliminate search and select therbligs.	Hands	Redesign layout
5	Optimize reach.	Hands	Redesign layout
6	Eliminate unscheduled rest stops due to fatigue.	Hands	Redesign layout and/or tools

Figure 6.1   Universal Motion Improvement Strategies Summary list.

However, I certainly do not mean to imply that this list is by any means exhaustive, but I do think it is probably a fair start at an initial "80/20" list.

My six identified universal strategies are summarized in Figure 6.1. As noted in this figure, the various strategies are either predominantly foot- or hand-related. The identified strategies also involve two primary improvement techniques: redesigning the task (and associated task sequence) and/or redesigning the work setting layout where the task is being performed. Each motion improvement strategy is individually described in greater detail in the following six sections.

Minimize Feet-Related Transport Empty Steps

As much as possible, trucking companies always try to minimize the time that their trucks travel down the freeway empty (not carrying a paying load). Such transport empty trips, called *deadheading*, only add cost and wasted time. Human feet-related transport empty task steps do essentially the same thing. They waste time that, in turn, decreases work productivity. So, just like trucking companies, these types of steps should always be minimized, if not outright eliminated whenever possible.

Remember my coffee-pouring task in the previous chapter? I described two different task sequences. One sequence involved getting up from my chair in the living room, walking to the kitchen, retrieving the coffee pot, and returning back to the living room where I poured my wife's second cup of coffee. I then returned the coffee pot to the kitchen, and walked back to my chair in the living room.

The second task sequence involved taking my wife's coffee cup to the kitchen, poring coffee, and returning to the living room with a full cup of coffee. I labeled the first task sequence "coffee pot to coffee cup." The second sequence is labeled "coffee cup to coffee pot."

In the previous process task flow sheets in Chapter 5, I only used the generic step classification of "transport" to identify my feet-related walking steps. However, now I will subdivide this generic transport task step into the following four categories:

- *Transport empty over a short distance* (TE-SD), meaning that I am empty handed but moving only a few feet in distance.
- *Transport empty over a long distance* (TE-LD), signifying that I am not carrying anything, but moving a longer distance from the living room to the kitchen and vice versa.
- *Transport loaded over a short distance* (TL-SD), indicating that I am now carrying a coffee pot or a coffee cup (empty or full) a few feet in distance.
- *Transport loaded over a long distance* (TL-LD), involving moving from living room to kitchen and vice versa carrying either a coffee pot or coffee cup (empty or full).

Next, I re-create the process task analysis worksheets initially illustrated in Chapter 5 (refer to Figures 5.9 and 5.10) using these new transportation subcategories. Figure 6.2 depicts the "coffee pot to coffee cup" task sequence. Figure 6.3 captures the "coffee cup to coffee pot" sequence.

Finally, I calculate a new summary table, as shown in Figure 6.4, recording data only for the four new transportation step subcategories. What do you observe in Figure 6.4? First, note total transport time differences: 25 seconds in total transportation time for the "coffee cup to coffee pot" task sequence versus 42.1 seconds for the "coffee pot to coffee cup" sequence. Also note in the shorter 25-second task sequence that there are no transport empty, long distance (TE-LD) steps identified. However, in the longer 42.1-second task sequence, there are two such TE-LD steps. These two

TE-LD steps account for a total time of 21.2 seconds, representing essentially half the total cycle time for that "coffee pot to coffee cup" task sequence.

Although this time difference may seem trivial, in a highly repetitive task sequence, it represents a great deal of time. Cutting these 21.2-second TE-LD times in a work-related task can translate into huge savings when aggregated by the hour or day.

Step #	Step Description	Flow	Time (Secs)	Notes
1	Walk to kitchen (empty handed).	TE-LD	11.2	
2	Grasp and remove coffee pot from coffeemaker.	●	2.1	
3	Carry coffee pot back to living room.	TE-LD	9.9	
4	Pour coffee into coffee cup.	●	4.6	
5	Carry coffee pot back to kitchen.	TE-LD	10.3	
6	Place coffee pot in coffeemaker.	●	1.8	
7	Walk back to chair in living room and be seated.	TE-LD	10.7	
		Total	**50.6**	

Figure 6.2 "Coffee pot to coffee cup" process task analysis worksheet.

Step #	Step Description	Flow	Time (Secs)	Notes
1	Get up from chair and walk to wife's chair.	TE-SD	1.9	
2	Grasp and remove coffee cup.	●	1.4	
3	Carry empty coffee cup to coffeemaker in kitchen.	TL-LD	10.4	
4	Remove coffee pot and pour coffee into cup.	●	6.8	
5	Replace coffee pot in coffeemaker.	●	3.6	
6	Carry full coffee cup to wife in living room and place coffee cup on coffee table.	TL-LD	10.7	
7	Return to and be seated in chair.	TE-SD	1.9	
		Total	**36.7**	

Figure 6.3 "Coffee cup to coffee pot" process task analysis worksheet.

Step Type	Coffee Pot to Coffee Cup		Coffee Cup to Coffee Pot	
	# of Steps	Time (Secs)	#of Steps	Time (Secs)
TE-SD	0	0	2	3.8
TE-LD	2	21.9	0	0
TL-SD	0	0	0	0
TL-LD	2	20.2	2	21.2
Total	4	42.1	4	25.0

Figure 6.4   Comparative "coffee pouring" analysis summary table.

#	Step Description	Flow	Time (Min)	Notes
1	Walks to location of PM in building	➡	10	PM job begins
2	Performs PM-related work	●	30	Normal PM work
3	Walks back to maintenance van	➡	10	Van in parking lot
4	Searches for needed information to continue PM	◗	15	Looks for service manual
5	Walks back to PM location	➡	10	
6	Continues PM-related work	●	20	Normal PM work
7	Walks back to maintenance van	➡	10	
8	Searches for a replacement gasket to continue PM	◗	10	Not where it was thought to be
9	Walks back to PM location	➡	10	
10	Continues PM-related work	●	15	Normal PM work
11	Walks back to maintenance van	➡	10	
12	Searches for replacement filter to complete PM	◗	5	
13	Walks back to PM location	➡	10	
14	Completes PM-related work	●	15	Normal PM work
15	Walks back to maintenance van a final time	➡	10	PM job completed

Figure 6.5   Preventive maintenance (PM) process task analysis worksheet. Note identified transport empty steps.

Identifying feet-related transport empty task steps can sometimes also identify whole nonvalue-added minitask sequences. For example, in the process task analysis worksheet depicted Figure 6.5, three transport empty steps are circled (admittedly to identify them, you have to read the step description). The worksheet describes a preventive maintenance (PM) activity.

As depicted in the flow part of the worksheet and related step descriptions and notes, the maintenance worker is repeatedly interrupting the PM task that he is performing inside a building to return to his van located out in the parking lot to search for and retrieve needed parts and information. After finding what he needs, he then returns to resume the PM task. These non-value-adding task interruption "minisequences" are captured by the task step triad of *transport–delay–transport*, as circled in Figure 6.6.

Successfully eliminating these task "triad" interruptions was accomplished by developing a prepackaged PM service kit containing all needed task supplies, information, and tools. Issuing the prepackaged kits to maintenance workers saved, on average, some 90 minutes per PM activity; a huge savings when aggregated over weeks of PM-related work. Further, this time savings translated into an average labor cost savings of $45 per PM activity.

Accordingly, always be on the lookout for feet-related transport empty steps in a task sequence. Sometimes such steps are necessary, but often they can be completely eliminated. Additionally, these transport empty steps are

#	Step Description	Flow	Time (Min)	Notes
1	Walks to location of PM in building	➡	10	PM job begins
2	Performs PM-related work	●	30	Normal PM work
3	Walks back to maintenance van	➡	10	Van in parking lot
4	Searches for needed information to continue PM	◗	15	Looks for service manual
5	Walks back to PM location	➡	10	
6	Continues PM-related work	●	20	Normal PM work
7	Walks back to maintenance van	➡	10	
8	Searches for a replacement gasket to continue PM	◗	10	Not where it was thought to be
9	Walks back to PM location	➡	10	
10	Continues PM-related work	●	15	Normal PM work
11	Walks back to maintenance van	➡	10	
12	Searches for replacement filter to complete PM	◗	5	
13	Walks back to PM location	➡	10	
14	Completes PM-related work	●	15	Normal PM work
15	Walks back to maintenance van a final time	➡	10	PM job completed

Figure 6.6   Subsets of nonvalue-adding transportation-related steps.

sometimes "bundled" with other nonvalue-adding steps. In such instances, the entire bundle often can be eliminated. Remember in any motion-improvement effort, the goal is always to think micro small, and aggregate macro big.

Shorten Transport Distances

Stop by your favorite fast-food restaurant for lunch and order a cheeseburger, fries, and chocolate milkshake (admittedly not the healthiest meal in the world). After placing your order, watch as it is being prepared. Note three things:

1. Your "order" consists of different parts (cheeseburger–fries–milkshake) that all have to be processed (e.g., produced) and assembled.
2. These various process and assembly tasks are performed at different workstations (e.g., a French fry cooking workstation, a milkshake dispenser workstation, and a hamburger cooking and assembly workstation).
3. Finally, observe that restaurant employees are moving from workstation to workstation to assemble your order. In fact, they seem to be constantly moving from workstation to workstation.

Admittedly these individual moving distances are measured in only a few feet at a time, but, cumulatively, those individual "few feet" distances can aggregate into many transport-related miles. I once calculated that an employee in a somewhat similar setting walked some 380 miles in a year, taking over 135 paid labor hours to do so.

Think about those short, "few feet" distances for a moment. If we increase the distance between the French fry, milkshake, and hamburger workstations, nothing of value is added. Your French fries will not be crispier, nor will your hamburger be juicier. Neither will those longer distances speed up the preparation and assembly of your food order. As such, one often-used strategy to shorten task cycle times is to shorten feet-related transportation distances, especially between workstations.

Consider, for example, Figure 6.7. It is a graphical layout of a work setting that contains six individual workstations. The workstations are neatly lined up in two parallel rows. Supply cabinets also are positioned and aligned along one wall. This particular work setting processes and assembles

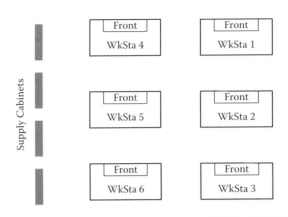

Figure 6.7   Initial workstation layout.

different work orders (much like the fast-food example above). Over twenty orders are processed each day, for a grand total of some 5,000 work orders per year.

However, not all workstations depicted in Figure 6.7 are involved in fulfilling each individual work order at a time. Involved workstations vary greatly per individual work order. Given this admittedly scant information, how would you go about analyzing and possibly improving the depicted workstation layout in Figure 6.7? Here is one suggested approach.

The filled-out work orders document and identify which workstations are involved in fulfilling each order and in what sequence they are used. This workstation-related type and sequence data represents a veritable motion-improvement gold mine and can be analyzed to better understand high- versus low-frequency workstation-to-workstation transport or human walking routes. Analyzing a year's worth of work order tickets indicates the following route information:

■ Route "workstation #1 to workstation #6" occurs 46 percent of the time.
■ Route "workstation #4 to workstation #6" occurs 28 percent of the time.
■ Route "workstation #2 to workstation #1 to workstation #6" occurs 16 percent of the time.
■ Route "workstation #5 to workstation #3" occurs 10 percent of the time.

These percentages are charted in a bar chart as illustrated in Figure 6.8. I next plot the routes on the original layout diagram, as graphically depicted in Figure 6.9.

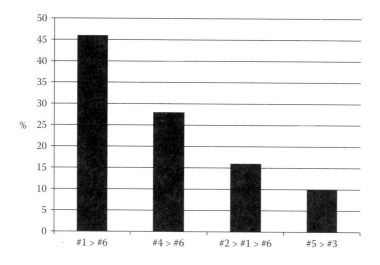

Figure 6.8   Workstation route frequency chart.

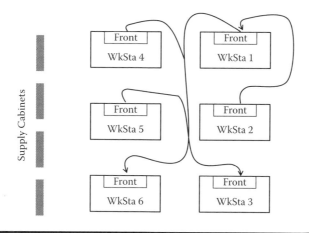

Figure 6.9   Original workstation-to-workstation transport routes.

Note in Figure 6.9 that the two highest frequency routes (#1 to #6 and #4 to #6) represent the *longest* walking distances. Also observe that going from workstation #2 to workstation #1 requires someone having to walk around to the front of the station.

Based on this analysis, the workstation layout is redesigned, as diagrammed in Figure 6.10. Three major changes are introduced:

- The *order* of the workstations is changed to better match frequency of use. For example, workstation #4 is now placed between workstations #5 and #6.

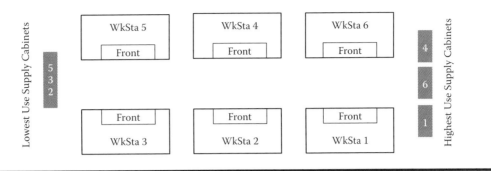

Figure 6.10 Redesigned workstation layout.

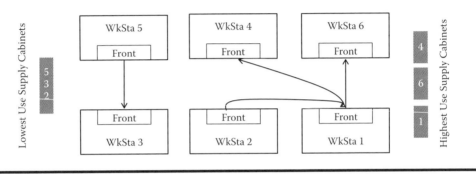

Figure 6.11 Workstation-to-workstation redesigned transport routes.

■ The workstations are placed in two parallel rows *facing* each other, with the two most frequently used stations, #6 and #1, situated directly opposite of each other.

■ The storage cabinets are moved as well. Three cabinets are now located on the right side of the room. These cabinets individually contain supplies for workstations #1, #6, and #4, respectively. This cabinet order represents the most frequent supply cabinet use. A larger storage cabinet is installed on the left side of the room, holding supplies for workstations #5, #3, and #2 in a clearly labeled and organized manner.

New transport routes are mapped on the redesigned layout, as depicted in Figure 6.11. Note the much shorter distances now travelled between machines by employees. Compare Figure 6.11 with Figure 6.9 to visually contrast these stark differences.

Following this relatively simple redesign effort, the manager of the operation and her employees were absolutely ecstatic with the new changes. One employee noted that her "feet" sensed a real difference after working just one day with the redesigned layout. When I asked the manager why the workstation layout was never changed, she stated truthfully that she had never really thought about making any changes. She said that the workstations were initially installed that way and that had always been "just the way it was."

Note, however, that with just a bit of systematic analysis and an improvement strategy of reconfiguring and shortening transport routes based on use volume frequencies, what a marked improvement it made. Also, this particular improvement effort did not require buying anything new; just, if you will, rearranging the furniture a bit. So, when it comes to human motion analysis and improvement, always think about shortening transport distances. In this instance, longer is not better, but shorter is.

Avoid Avoidable Delays

When you focus on observing hands and feet while someone is performing a task, you normally see lots of motion. Some of it is value-added and some of it is not. However, sometimes you see no movement at all. The hands and feet are still. There may be a perfectly good and justified reason for this observed lack of motion, but oftentimes such stillness signifies some type of task delay, and most delays are nonvalue-adding. About the only thing they do is consume time, which, in turn, lengthens cycle time (while also lowering productivity and increasing operating costs).

Frank Gilbreth (see Chapter 1) identified two types of delays: avoidable and unavoidable. An *avoidable delay* is a delay or standby motion that can be completely eliminated if the right kind of change or improvement is made in a task sequence. An *unavoidable delay* is a delay caused by something for which the person performing the task is not responsible (e.g., it is beyond that person's control). In some task sequences requiring multiple workers to perform a task, unavoidable delays are purposely built into the task sequence. However, in those specific instances, not all workers should be unavoidably delayed at the same time. Indeed, some workers in a given task setting should never be delayed, either unavoidably or avoidably.

Consider, for example, a NASCAR pit crew changing tires during a race (ignore for now the guy filling up the racecar's gas tank). These tire changing individuals include:

■ *One jack man*: The jack man carries a 20-pound hydraulic jack and raises the car on both sides—first right, then left—to allow the tires to be changed.

■ *Two tire carriers*: Starting on the right side of the car and repeating the process on the left side, the two tire carriers (one each for front and back tires) carry new tires over the pit wall and hand them to the tire changers.

■ *Two tire changers*: Each tire changer first removes and replaces a right-side tire (front and back) using an air-powered impact wrench to loosen and tighten five lug nuts holding the tire rim in place. They then move to the opposite side of the car to change the left-side front and rear tires.

In this five-man, tire-changing work crew, consider the jack man first. After he jacks up the car, he has to wait a few seconds (an unavoidable delay) as one side of the car's tires is changed. Similarly, the two tire carriers also have unavoidable delays of a few seconds each as they wait for their respective tire changer to remove a tire. However, in this task sequence, the tire changers should *never* have any type of delay—unavoidable or avoidable. The two tire changers represent the proverbial "long pole in the tent." The speed of their movements determines the speed or time of the entire tire change task sequence, and essentially that of the pit stop itself.

Accordingly, when analyzing and trying to improve any task sequence, always try to:

■ minimize (if not outright eliminate them) all unavoidable delays
■ eliminate (seek and destroy) all avoidable delays

The key to eliminating avoidable and unavoidable delays is in first identifying them and then determining why they occur in the first place. Examine Figure 6.12. Note the top process task step flow consists of the following four steps: transport (arrow), operation (circle), transport, and operation.

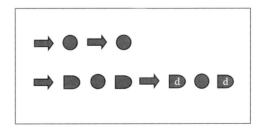

Figure 6.12 Two differing task sequences without (top) and with (bottom) embedded delays.

Now compare this upper task step sequence with the lower one. Note the delay steps (stretched out Ds) bracketing each operation step. Whenever you see a "delay-plagued" task sequence like this, determine why such delays are present and then eliminate their occurrence.

Similar delays can occur in hand micromotions. Assume, for example, that someone is using a hand tool. Note the following therblig motion sequence:

$$TE > G > TL + P > AD > U$$

Do you spot anything wrong? Hopefully you identified the Type 3 motion therblig, "avoidable delay" or AD. It occurs just before the "use" therblig (U). Sometimes when I see this AD occurrence just prior to "use," it is because the person is unfamiliar with exactly how to use the tool (a knowledge and skill problem).

At other times, however, it is because the tool has been improperly positioned *to use*. In this case, and if you look very closely, you will actually observe the following therblig sequence:

$$TE > G > TL + P > AD > TL + P > U$$

Note, in this instance, that the second "transport loaded plus position" or "TL + P" therblig combination is like a rework step. It is repeating and correcting an earlier "TL + P" motion.

Avoidable delays also may occur just before the "assemble" or "disassemble" therbligs (AD > A or AD > DA). The cause for this observation is basically the same as above—a lack of understanding or poor hand or tool positioning. In some instances, poor positioning, in turn, may be a "reach" problem, which will be discussed later.

So, when it comes to either foot- or hand-associated delays, the improvement strategy is simple. Always try to eliminate all avoidable delays. If unavoidable delays cannot be avoided, then reduce their time durations to the absolute minimum.

Eliminate Search and Select Therbligs

I once bought three large workbenches to go into a new garage and shop complex that we had just finished building. The workbenches had to be assembled prior to placing them in the new shop. To assemble the workbenches required dealing with a very large number of bolts and nuts of four differing sizes. The different-sized bolts and nuts came in their own individual packages. Being concerned that I might lose a bolt or nut, and was not sure if extras were provided, I came up with the brilliant idea of dumping all the bolts and nuts into a large can for safekeeping.

As I began to follow the assembly instructions, each step called for a different-sized nut and bolt. I would read the specific step instruction and then paw through the can looking for the right-sized bolt and nut. Once selected, it was quite easy to insert the bolt and tighten the nut (an assembly therblig). Because a number of bolts and nuts were required for each single step, I was continuously moving my hand back and forth to the can to find another right-sized bolt and nut.

From a therblig perspective, my right-handed repetitive motions looked something like this:

$$St > G > TL + P > A > St > G > TL + P > A > St > G > TL$$
$$+ P > A > St > G > TL + P > A$$

Note that in this larger therblig motion sequence, each subsequence (St > G > TL + P > A) begins with the therblig select or "St" and ends with the assemble (A) motion.

Remember from the previous chapter that the "search" therblig can be incorporated into the "select" motion. In this search–select combination, select now refers to the hunting and locating of one object from among several objects, or, in my case, the hunting and locating of one-sized bolt and nut among a can full of differing-sized bolts and nuts. At this higher combination level, "St" begins when the eyes and/or hands begin to hunt for the object and ends when the desired object has been located (usually just immediately prior to "grasp"). With this broader definition of select, moving an empty hand forward (transport empty) is now incorporated into the "select" motion.

So, in "therblig speak," I was doing this: St > G > TL + P > A, instead of doing this: TE > G > TL + P > A. And, I soon realized that doing this St > G > TL + P > A therblig thing was taking an inordinate amount of (wasted) time.

Becoming a bit smarter on the assembly of the next two workbenches, I put all same-sized nuts and bolts into separate cans and clearly labeled each can. This before-and-after can-related improvement strategy is graphically depicted in Figure 6.13. The difference in resultant assembly times based on this simple change was amazing. Although I had certainly become

Figure 6.13   Before and after can-related improvement strategy.

more knowledgeable in "how" to assemble the workbenches, resulting by itself in faster assembly cycle times, the elimination of the "select" therblig was equally, if not more, valuable in reducing assembly times.

These changes may seem like a very simple and obvious improvement strategy, and admittedly they are. Yet, shortly after I had completed my home workbench assembly tasks, I happened to be on a business trip in a different state. Part of that business trip involved visiting two small manufacturing and assembly shops. In both shops, I observed someone assembling a large component. In the first shop, the assembler was repeatedly "selecting" or pawing through a large bucket filled with different-sized bolts, nuts, and screws. He reminded me of myself.

However, in the second shop that I visited, things were decidedly different. Everything in the shop was extremely well organized, and, sure enough, the person assembling the large component was moving his hand directly (no "select" motions here) to a separate and clearly labeled can containing only a single-sized bolt. Right next to that bolt can was another can containing the associated same-sized nut; same-sized bolt and same-sized nut in two different but adjacent and clearly labeled cans. The contrast between these two shops was striking.

The very act of searching for something implies that we cannot immediately find that something. That is, we are having trouble perceiving or detecting something per the described PCA (perception–cognition–action) cycle. Remember what Kato (1991) said about the search therblig:

■ It is *not* a search if a person already knows what the object he or she is looking for and its approximate location.
■ Conversely, it is a search if the person knows what the object he or she is looking for is, but *does not* know its location.

When we cannot find our car keys, for example, we know what we are looking for (our car keys), but we do not know their approximate location. If we did know their approximate location, it would not be "search."

The problem with searching for something is that it unnecessarily consumes task cycle time, even if that consumed time is measured in mere seconds. Thus, the question is: How do you eliminate search and select? The answer is: By establishing a set location for everything and when necessary, clearly labeling that location.

For example, if you walk down the hallway of a hospital, you often find a "crash cart" parked against the wall. If a patient's heart stops beating or if the patient stops breathing, then he instantly needs the crash cart. The crash cart contains all sorts of stuff to treat a medical emergency in a clearly detectable manner—no search or select is required here.

Therefore, the key to eliminating search and select is organization and associated labeling, and constancy of placement (e.g., always placing the crash cart and its various components in the exact same location). For example, if I need a measuring spoon, I know instantly that all measuring spoons are located in the second drawer to the left of the kitchen sink. I also know that they are located on the left side of that second drawer. The drawer is neatly organized (thanks to my wife) and there is a constancy of placement; the measuring cups are always located there.

Return to the earlier redesigned layout in Figure 6.11. Part of that redesign effort involved moving the storage cabinets to opposite sides of the room. One set of newly placed storage cabinets contains supplies for the most frequently used workstations, in this case workstations #1, #6, and #4. They also have been relocated immediately next to those three machines, permitting easy reach. Admittedly, all of these changes are little stuff, but when it comes to improving human performance, it is the little stuff that counts. So, to eliminate nonvalue-adding time and wasteful search and select motions, think about organization and associated labeling, and constancy of placement. Now, if we could just do the same thing for our car keys and cell phone.

Optimize Reach

Remember Frank Gilbreth's improvement strategy for increasing the number of bricks his bricklayers could lay? That strategy was threefold and involved:

- Identifying and then eliminating wasted motions and steps associated with the laying of each brick.
- Rearranging the placement of the bricks and mortar to a more accessible and easily reachable location.

■ Redesigning the scaffolding to increase brick-laying speed and reduce worker fatigue.

Note the second strategy involved rearranging the placement of the bricks and mortar to a more accessible and easily *reachable* location. Gilbreth understood the importance of "reach" when it comes to manually working with our hands. *Reach* involves making a movement or motion with one's hand(s) and arm(s) to touch or grasp something. When it comes to reach, the improvement strategy is simple: optimize reach, which normally involves shortening it. That is, rearrange all critically needed tools, parts, materials, etc., to a more accessible and easily reachable position.

Obviously we cannot always place "everything" we might need to complete a task in an immediately reachable position. In those instances when we cannot place everything in an immediately reachable position, we need to prioritize the placement of objects. For example, if you are building a brick wall, bricks and mortar are critical items. Hence, they should definitely be placed in the most reachable position possible. Perhaps a rarely used bricklaying tool can be placed "out of reach," but, in a clearly designated and nonsearch required location. A good way to identify what items represent the "bricks and mortar" of a particular task sequence is via frequency charts, just like the one I used in Figure 6.8. In this instance, higher frequency-used objects should always be placed closer to a person and in a more reachable manner.

Think of a person sitting at a workbench, as illustrated in Figure 6.14. In this illustration, the person is represented by the oval in the figure. As seen in the figure, a "normal" hand reach is approximately a 15-inch distance from the center of the seated body. Those 15 inches represent an immediate or normal working space distance. A maximum reachable working space distance as depicted in Figure 6.15 is about 25 inches. Thinking in terms of these normal and maximum reachable working distances, one should design

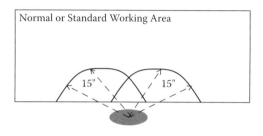

Figure 6.14   Fifteen-inch hand reach in normal working area.

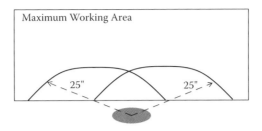

Figure 6.15   Twenty-five-inch hand reach in maximum working area.

a work area accordingly. In an optimally designed individual work area, all objects (tools, parts, supplies, etc.) would be arranged and organized in such a way that the most frequently used objects are placed and neatly organized within the most immediate and reachable position (within 15 inches). Needed secondary items then would be placed in the more extended, 25-inch "reachable" area.

Making hand-held objects more reachable and findable accomplishes two positive things in parallel:

1. It eliminates Type 2 search and select motions that only add wasteful time to Type 1 motions.
2. It lessens worker fatigue, making work easier and more productive.

Thus, optimizing reach *and* eliminating search and select therbligs often go together. One enables the other, and both significantly reduce task cycle times. Therefore, the next time you observe a work area cluttered and poorly organized with lousy reach distances, think about wasteful Type 2 and Type 3 therblig motions. These wasted motions, in turn, translate into longer than necessary task cycle times and increased worker fatigue.

Eliminate Unscheduled Fatigue-Caused Rest

Note the following therblig motion sequence: TL + P > U > R > U > R. What do you observe? Hopefully a number of "Rs" interspersed between "Us." Or numerous nonvalue-adding Type 3 unscheduled "rest" stops intermingled between value-adding Type 1 "use" motions.

This minitask sequence indicates that the person using the object (such as a tool) is unable to sustain that action until the particular task step is successfully completed. In turn, this observation normally suggests one of two things:

1. The person does not have the requisite physical capacity to perform the "use" motion—an individual differences issue.
2. The object or tool is poorly designed and cannot be used in a sustainable manner by the average worker.

The first reason is a personnel selection issue. The second reason, however, deals with the design of the tool itself and represents an ergonomics issue. The solution to this second issue is to either get a new and less fatiguing tool, or, if one is not available, then to redesign the existing tool. Remember how Gilbreth redesigned his scaffolding to increase bricklaying speed and *reduce* worker fatigue. The same concept holds true here.

Although specific tool redesign techniques and related ergonomic remedies are beyond the scope of this book, they should always be considered. If an observed task sequence identifies unscheduled fatigue-caused rest stops, then their cause and elimination should become a high priority. In some instances, a poorly designed tool or other "object" can not only cause fatigue and resultant unscheduled rest stops, but also result in worker injury. This latter observation is especially true if tool or other object use occurs in a highly repeated and repetitive manner over prolonged periods of time.

For example, carpal tunnel syndrome refers to swelling and pressure in the wrist and hand areas caused by repetitive strain injuries. The carpal arch and flexor retinaculum delimit a narrow space called the carpal tunnel. Within the carpal tunnel passes the median nerve and tendons of the hand flexor muscles. It is damage to the nerve and tendons that causes carpal tunnel syndrome.

Carpal tunnel syndrome injuries are extremely painful and often require corrective surgery. However, in some instances, even having corrective surgery does not completely alleviate the pain or problem. In such instances, the affected person may be unable to safely perform the same job again.

The goal in dealing with repetitive strain injuries is to not have to surgically "fix" the problem. Rather, it is to prevent their occurrence in the first place. For a much more comprehensive and excellent treatment of the whole field of ergonomics, I strongly suggest reading the second edition of *Ergonomics: How to Design for Ease and Efficiency* by Kroemer et al. (2000).

In summary, improving motion-related human performance often involves doing a number of small things that accumulate over time in some very big ways, particularly in terms of decreased task cycle times and associated cost savings and increases in productivity. The key in such improvement efforts is to think "feet" and "hands." Eliminate or shorten feet steps, avoid avoidable delays, organize and redesign work settings to eliminate unnecessary search, optimize hand reach, and reduce worker fatigue at both the macro and micro levels.

ANALYZING AND IMPROVING HUMAN-RELATED QUALITY AND SAFETY

The human factor is always the most important in any engineering project.

—Douglas Preston and Lincoln Child
The Lost Island

Chapter 7

Human Error Analysis

A human error analysis is often performed following a mishap. In certain instances, that mishap may involve a quality-related issue in which human error seems to be a contributing factor. In other instances, such analyses are often associated with some type of formal or informal, internal or external accident investigation.

The level of intensity or sophistication of a human error analysis is routinely a function of the resultant consequences of the adverse event itself. In this usage, an *adverse event* is defined as an unwanted incident with real or potential negative consequences. An adverse event refers to the spectrum of unintended *and* intended undesired incidents, including:

- Accidents (and near misses)
- Quality problems
- Severe natural phenomena
- Financial adversities
- Political adversities
- Security breaches (including terrorist attacks)

My primary focus in this chapter is on accidents and quality-related issues that involve some aspect of human error. However, the same types of analyses are equally applicable to many other adverse event occurrences (e.g., financial).

Adverse events occur in what I describe as an organization's "failure space" (depicted in Chapter 1, Figure 1.2). Such failure events can have varying degrees of consequence "magnitude." Caution, however, must be used in assessing consequence magnitude. In some instances, differences between supposedly high- and low-consequence events may simply be more luck and happenstance than anything else.

For example, my wife and I live on a large ranch complex in the mountains of southern Colorado. At one time in the early 1900s, the surrounding area was a major producer of coking or metallurgical coal used in making steel. Numerous underground coal mines (now all closed) dot the region and some of these mines suffered catastrophic explosions, which were primarily caused by deadly mixtures of methane gas and coal dust. However, not all explosions, even those of similar amplitude, resulted in the same loss of life.

One mine to the northeast of us suffered a catastrophic explosion in the middle of the night. Huge timbers were reportedly propelled down the mine workings for a hundred yards or more. Because of the time of the explosion (the middle of the night) only two men were killed. By comparison, another mine to the southwest of us suffered a similar, if not less-order amplitude explosion. Because that explosion occurred during the day shift when the mine was full of working miners, 263 men were killed (representing the second worse recorded coal mining disaster in the United States). As illustrated, differing consequences can mask similar, if not identical, underlying causes.

Techniques for conducting a human error analysis are explored in the following three sections. In the first section, a general analytical methodology is introduced. Unfortunately, I have learned the hard way that when it comes to accident investigations, methodology matters. Author John Barry (2005) does a superb job summarizing the importance of a selected methodology when he observes that "… the way one goes about answering a question, one's methodology, matters as much as the question itself. … That is, how one pursues a question often dictates or, at the very least, limits the answer." The methodology presented in the first section provides a structured, yet flexible framework for pursuing human error-related questions.

The second section illustrates how to apply the described analytical methodology with a detailed case study, which involves a partial analysis of a horrific military friendly fire incident in Iraq. Finally, the third section provides a series of what I term *pointer questions*, based on the previously developed perception–cognition–action or PCA cycle. Whenever I am conducting a human error analysis, I always carry these questions with me and have found them to be great reminders regarding questions to ask and avenues to explore.

Methodology

Admittedly, when I first began investigating adverse events as a human performance specialist, I was not nearly as well prepared as I could or should have been. Following some of my earlier investigations, I had too many leftover "I should have asked that …" questions still needing answered. I also quickly learned from these earlier experiences that incident investigations are rather chaotic and almost always stressful and time-constrained. I further discovered that no two investigations are ever exactly alike. To counter these investigation realities and some of my own admitted shortcomings, I started to develop a more flexible methodology that I could apply in almost any adverse event setting. Over the years, the developed methodology or investigative framework has stood the test of time and seems to work fairly well.

My derived methodology consists of five general and somewhat sequential investigative "parts," involving:

1. Obtaining some initial *general background information*, helping to set the stage of the incident. If possible, I try to collect this general background information before arriving onsite of an event investigation.
2. Developing a detailed *event chronology*, focusing on *what* happened *when* and *where*, and *who* was specifically involved at the when and where. This *who* identification, however, never attempts to place blame or responsibility. Its purpose is to only identify all of the "actors" involved in the event. The goal of step #2 is to be as factual and objective as possible. I also have found that developing this event chronology as soon as possible after an incident has occurred is extremely important.
3. The identification of differing "confounding variables." This portion of the investigation attempts to identify all associated *latent factors* and related *error-producing conditions* that directly or indirectly may have influenced the event, or negatively affected certain involved actors, thereby increasing the probability of human errors. As described in Chapter 4, Williams' HEART technique involving identifying error-producing conditions is of particular value here. The goal of step #3 is

to end up with a list and associated description of all pertinent latent factors, including all identified error-producing conditions. This list, in turn, helps me prepare for the fourth, really interesting part of the methodology.

4. Armed with a preliminary understanding of the event, including a detailed event chronology and identified latent factors and error-producing conditions list, I next attempt to re-create the event chronology developed in part #2 through the eyes of each major actor who was involved in the incident. That is, by *looking from the inside of the event outward.* As noted, I frequently find this "re-creating" portion of the analysis to be the most interesting part of any human error investigation, often providing a number of unexpected insights and findings. In many instances, obvious and so-called "stupid errors" often become much less obvious and "stupid" when viewed through the eyes of the person making them, and at the time they were being made. In point of fact, I have often found myself saying that given those exact same conditions, I would have probably acted (e.g., performed) in the exact same manner.

5. My final step of any investigation is *interpretation.* This investigative portion is often completed away from the actual event scene and just prior to the final report write-up. In this final interpretation part of the investigation, I attempt to understand how embedded latent factors and associated error-producing conditions—the context—may have conspired to negatively affect human performance, particularly among the chief actors.

A human error analysis and a human motion analysis are similar in that they both involve the systematic and objective collection of data. However, in a human error analysis associated with an accident investigation, these collected data are often referred to as "evidence." Such collected evidence may include:

■ Personnel interviews
■ Recordings and transcripts of actual verbal communications
■ Video and still photos, especially video from security cameras
■ Event walk downs (observing where and how the event occurred through space and time)
■ Re-enactments of the event itself (if possible)
■ Inspections of physical components involved in the event, especially those that might have failed
■ Work procedure, work policy, and other work instruction-type reviews

I further divide these various types of evidence into two broad categories:

- Hard evidence
  - Recordings and transcripts
  - Video and still photos
  - Physical component damage
- Soft evidence
  - Interviews
  - "Eyewitness" accounts
  - Walk downs and event reenactments

Each general hard and soft evidence category has its own set of plusses and minuses. Some of these plusses and minuses include:

- Hard evidence
  - Often tells a very accurate, but limited part of the story.
  - Usually needs some interpretation.
  - Never seems to exist exactly where and when you need it the most.
- Soft evidence
  - Usually much more abundant than hard evidence.
  - May or may not tell an accurate part of the story.
  - Problems with story creep and story improvement over time. This observation is especially true if someone thinks that he/she might get into trouble as a result of the event.
  - Conflicting stories between various observers and/or event actors.
  - "Sooner interviews" that are recorded immediately after an event are normally more informative and factual than later ones. However, sometimes later, "I forgot about that …" information can be extremely valuable from previously interviewed personnel.

In conducting a human error analysis, especially one involved in a more formal incident investigation, I offer the following advice:

- Always stick to the facts, continuously adding more and more detail. However, adding increasing detail is almost always an iterative process, but that is okay. Do not be afraid to go backwards, forwards, and backwards again (e.g., from step #4 back to step #3 or #2). The important point is collecting sound evidence that adds up to a better understanding of the event. Although people might disagree with your interpretation, they should generally agree with your collected facts, such as your developed event chronology in step #2.

■ Do not jump to premature conclusions or make unnecessary first-day preliminary statements. Often such early and hasty statements can come back to haunt you, especially if you change them later (which you almost always will). By not providing preliminary thoughts or too early interpretations, you can avoid the "But, you earlier said ..." accusations.

■ Do not reconstruct an event simply to fit an already preconceived notion or an earlier formed and potentially biased interpretation. That is why sticking to the facts is so important; they keep you and everyone else honest.

■ Do not ignore conflicting evidence. Instead, continue your investigation and resolve all identified conflicts. People always view things differently, especially under stressful conditions. That is why the construction of a detailed, accurate, and fact-based event chronology is so important. It is one way of judging the veracity of differing observations.

■ When conducting an interview, empower the person being interviewed, especially if that person is an incident "actor." For example, at the start of every interview, I always state that I will be taking notes. I then invite the person that I am interviewing to also take notes if he or she wishes to do so. Although I have never had anyone accept this offer, it seems to set the stage of two "equals" discussing the event, lowering the potential stress of the interview a bit.

■ Unfortunately, any after-the-fact or retrospective analysis is always fraught with potential bias. Knowing the outcome *before* putting the whole story together can easily lead one astray. So, as much as humanly possible, become one with the event actors, attempting to envision an event solely through their eyes. Try to imagine what those actors saw and heard and, just as importantly, what they did not see and hear; what they might have thought they saw and heard and what it all meant to them at the time of the event, not after the event. And, based on what they saw and what they thought it all meant, why they selected a specific action over other, possible alternative actions.

■ Finally, be wary of hidden agendas, especially when someone says, "I knew that guy was bad from the start ..." Personality differences should never play a role in any incident investigation, unless those differences had a direct effect on the incident itself.

As an investigation progresses, I often begin developing what I term my "million dollar question" list. These questions, always just a few in number, usually take the form of: "Why did ..." or "Why didn't ..." somebody do something or something happened. Answering such questions can often provide a great deal of insight into an event, unlocking many of the mysteries surrounding the event itself. Crime novelist Michael Connelly (2012) captures this sentiment perfectly in the novel *The Box* in reference to ace detective Harry Bosch. Bosch believes that every case "... had a black box; a piece of evidence, a person, a positioning of facts that brought a certain understanding and helped explain what happened and why." So always look for the black box, both literally and figuratively.

A partial analysis of a major adverse event is provided in the next section as an applied case study using the developed methodology. However, since it is only a partial analysis, I have not included the final and full interpretation component of the methodology. What is perhaps unique concerning this particular case study is the amount of "hard evidence" that is preserved. This preservation permits a much deeper understanding of the incident than is often afforded in other investigations that lack such evidence.

Snook (2000) makes an interesting observation about "big" accidents. According to Snook, if we could "... put together a library of such treasures (big accidents), thick behavioral descriptions of complex untoward events, I am confident that such studies will move us closer to unlocking the fundamental design mysteries of hypercomplex organizations." Snook identifies this friendly fire incident as one such "big accident."

Case Study

On April 14, 1994, two U.S. Army UH-60 Black Hawk helicopters carrying a multinational contingent of VIPs were mistakenly shot down by two U.S. Air Force F-15C fighter jets in the northern no-fly zone of Iraq. Both helicopters were destroyed and all 26 personnel onboard were killed. The tragedy represents the worst U.S. friendly fire incident since World War II.

A partial analysis of the incident is provided here. Particular attention is given to better understanding the ensuing shoot down through the eyes of the two involved F-15 pilots. For more in-depth analyses of the tragedy, the reader is referred to the work of Diehl (2002); Ladkin and Stuphan (2003); Leveson, Allen, and Storey (2002); Piper (2001); Snook (2000; 2001); and a U.S. General Accounting Office report (1997). The book *Friendly Fire* by

Snook (2000) is especially insightful and is highly recommended. Note that a U.S. Air Force officer who was involved in the actual investigation following the tragedy has reviewed this analysis for accuracy.

General Background Information

Immediately following the successful 1991 U.S.-led coalition victory in the first Gulf War, two no-fly zones were established within Iraq. One zone was located in the southern portion of the country and a second was located to the north, immediately above the 36th parallel and ending at the Turkish border. Protecting the airspace of the northern no-fly zone and the resident Kurdish population fell under the operational auspices of *Operation Provide Comfort*. The actual no-fly zone was designated the Tactical Area of Responsibility or TAOR, and will hereinafter be referred to as such. Within the TAOR was a special security zone, set up specifically to offer enhanced protection to Kurdish residents. Additionally, three towns are referenced in the case study as identified in Figure 7.1: *Incirlik* in Turkey, and *Zakhu* and *Irbil* in Iraq.

Up until the day of the incident, *Operation Provide Comfort* had been underway for 1,103 days without an accident. This supposedly stellar safety record included over 5,000 flight hours and some 1,400 successful helicopter flights into the TAOR region.

It also is important to note that on the day of the event, only four aircraft were flying in Iraqi TAOR airspace (the two Black Hawk helicopters and two F-15C fighter planes), all communicating with the same E-3B Airborne Warning and Control System (AWACS) plane that was flying in Turkish airspace. Additionally, all four aircraft were flying in broad daylight with

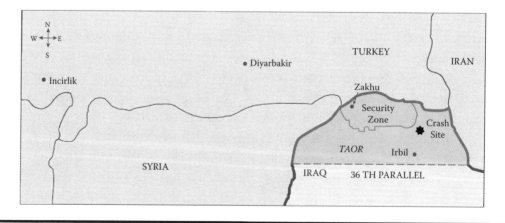

Figure 7.1 TAOR in the Iraqi northern no-fly zone.

unlimited visibility. Operational conditions at the time of the incident were exceedingly benign, with no Clausewitzian "fog of war." Nor was there any enemy fire present that often characterizes other friendly fire incidents.*

Event Chronology

The following chronology delineates the sequence of major events that occurred on the morning of April 14, 1994. Note that times are expressed as Zulu or military time. The developed event chronology is primarily based on recorded aircraft communications between the F-15 lead pilot and the AWACS aircraft. This communication data represents "hard evidence" as described in the previous section.

> *0436*: An E-3B AWACS plane departs Incirlik Air Base in Turkey and pro-
> ceeds to fly eastward to an area just north of the TAOR in Iraq, while
> still remaining in Turkish-protected airspace (see Figure 7.2).
>
> *0545*: AWACS plane reports "on station" to aircraft control personnel at
> Incirlik Air Base. It then commences to fly a racetrack pattern to pro-
> vide constant surveillance and control of coalition flights flying into
> and out of the TAOR region. The AWACS onboard enroute controller is
> responsible for controlling all fixed-wing flights inside Turkey airspace.
> Once those flights enter into the no-fly zone, however, the AWACS
> onboard TAOR controller assumes flight control responsibility.

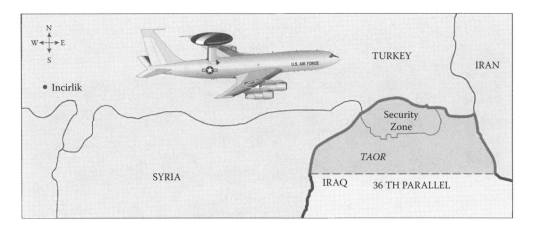

Figure 7.2   AWACS flight in Turkey airspace.

---

* Carl von Clausewitz was a German (Prussian) general and military theorist who wrote *Vom Kriege* (On War).

0635: Two F-15C fighter jets depart Incirlik Air Base. They are supposedly the first aircraft that will enter TAOR airspace that morning. Their assigned mission is to sanitize the area prior to subsequent coalition flights scheduled throughout the rest of the day. The two F-15s are authorized to shoot down any Iraqi aircraft that may be encountered during their initial sweep of the area (see Figure 7.3).

0715: F-15 lead pilot checks in with the onboard AWACS Air Command Element (ACE) prior to entering TAOR airspace. He requests "words" or any new updates. ACE replies "negative words," signifying no new updates.

0720: F-15s enter TAOR airspace and the lead pilot notifies the AWACS TAOR controller of current position.

0722: F-15 lead pilot notifies AWACS TAOR controller of an unidentified radar contact inside the TAOR that represents a low flying, slow-moving target. AWACS controller responds "clean there," indicating that there are no known radar contacts in the vicinity of the unidentified target.

0723: F-15s interrogate unidentified target with Identify Friend or Foe (IFF) system on both Mode 1 and Mode IV (the backup or safety channel). Both interrogations are negative (no friendly response). Note that both F-15s had switched their IFF Mode I code from 43 to 52 upon entering TAOR airspace. All friendly fixed-wing aircraft flying in Turkey on April 14, 1994, flew with Mode I coded 43. Upon entering the TAOR, they switched to Mode I coded 52 per standard flight procedures.

0724: F-15s move to unidentified target location to initiate a visual identification (VID) pass.

0725: Enroute to VID, F-15 lead pilot reports second radar contact to AWACS TAOR controller. AWACS TAOR controller replies "hits there,"

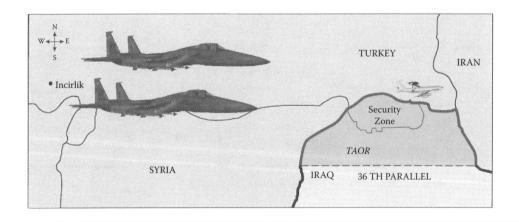

Figure 7.3   F-15 fighter jets enroute to TAOR airspace.

signifying an unidentified contact is now displayed on the controller's screen as well. An AWACS response of "paint there" or "green there" would have indicated to the F-15 pilots that the contacts were friendly. "Hits there" signifies radar contact is unidentified.

0726: F-15 lead pilot executes a VID pass at approximately 450 knots.

0728: F-15 lead pilot has a "visual" at five nautical miles and closes in to pass above and behind the targets that are flying approximately 200 feet above the ground. F-15 lead plane flies at some 500 feet above the target and 1,000 feet off to the target's right. F-15 lead pilot reports: "Tally two Hinds," signifying that he has identified two Iraqi helicopter Mi-24 Hind gunships (a Russian-manufactured assault helicopter). AWACS TAOR controller replies, "Copy Hinds," acknowledging enemy aircraft identification.

0728.5: F-15 wing or second pilot conducts independent VID and calls out: "Tally Two."

0729: F-15 lead pilot calls AWACS TAOR controller and reports: "Cougar (AWACS call sign), Tiger 02 (call sign for F-15 wing pilot) has tallied two Hinds, engaged."

0729+: F-15 lead pilot orders targeting and instructs his wing pilot to "arm hot." He further executes a final Mode I Identify Friend or Foe check, but once again receives a negative response ("no friendly" response).

0730: F-15 lead pilot fires a missile at trail target from approximately four miles out. Immediately following the lead pilot's missile, the F-15 wing pilot fires a second missile at the lead target from approximately two miles out.

0730+: F-15 lead pilot reports, "Splash two Hinds," indicating that both targets were successfully hit and destroyed.

Unbeknownst to the two F-15 pilots, two U.S. Army UH-60 Black Hawks carrying a multinational contingent of VIPs bound for Irbil, a village located deep inside the no-fly zone (refer to Figure 7.1 for location), had entered TAOR airspace at 0621 that morning. The Black Hawk helicopters had reported their location to the same AWACS plane that would later control the F-15 flight. Unbeknownst to the two F-15 pilots, the two VIP helicopters had received a special U.S. Air Force exemption the day before to enter the TAOR *prior* to the April 14 morning F-15 sweep.

Compounding Factors

During the ensuing investigation, a number of compounding factors were identified. Many of these identified factors represent embedded latent factors, including a number of error-producing conditions as described in Chapter 4.

A partial list of some of these factors is provided here. Pay particular attention to the earlier observation in Chapter 4 that sometimes under the right conditions, simple mistakes and systemic organizational weaknesses combine with deadly consequences.

- *UH-60 Black Hawk Flight*: On the day before the helicopter flight, the army had received an exemption from the air force to enter the TAOR prior to the morning's sweep by the two F-15 fighter jets. This exemption was in direct violation of an Air Force Airspace Control Order that specifically mandated that *no aircraft* would enter the no-fly zone until jet fighters had sanitized or cleared the area. Yet, supposedly on previous occasions, helicopters had entered the TAOR under just such conditions. Additionally on this particular day, the two Black Hawk helicopters were bound for Irbil, a village located deep inside the TAOR. Such long flights were infrequent, but not uncommon. Of some 1,400 *Operation Provide Comfort* (OPC) helicopter flights, 95 percent of the time they penetrated TAOR airspace no more than 300 meters during their flight to the small village of Zakhu that housed the headquarters of the Military Coordination Center.

- *E-3 AWACS Initial Flight*: April 14, 1994, marked the first day that the AWACS crew had flown together in-theater. AWACS aircrews were routinely shuttled in and out of theater operations on a 30-day rotational schedule, so, over the course of OPC, there had been many "first day" AWACS flights. To ensure a smooth transition during changeovers, experienced "shadow" personnel initially accompanied all new flight crews.

- *E-3 AWACS Wake-Up Orbit*: On the morning's initial outbound leg, the AWACS crew performs what is called a "wake-up orbit" in which it brings all systems online and performs a series of premission tests and checks. On this particular day, the enroute controller's radar console was inoperative. To accommodate such infrequent but not uncommon contingencies, spare radar consoles are available. Accordingly, the enroute controller, who normally sat between the Tanker and TAOR controllers and directly faced the senior director, moved to a spare seat and console directly behind and facing away from the senior director.

- *Helicopter Flight Handoff at TAOR*: While in Turkish airspace, the Black Hawk helicopter flight was handled by the enroute controller. Upon entering TAOR airspace and per procedure, helicopter flights should have been handed off to the TAOR controller. Additionally, the helicopters should have changed radio frequencies and IFF Mode I code.

This was standard practice for all fixed wing aircraft. However, it was normal practice to treat helicopter flights differently and *not* to hand them off to the TAOR controller per procedure. As such, helicopter flights remained under the control of the enroute controller, even while they were in TAOR airspace. This practice, although against established procedure, actually made sense in that 95 percent of the time helicopter flights penetrated TAOR airspace no more than 300 meters on their frequent flights to Zakhu. According to Snook (2000), there are "… written rules and there are emergent rules." For 95 percent of the time, it made a great deal of sense not to switch controllers and was probably even a safer practice from a helicopter flight crew workload perspective. Unfortunately, on this particular day, the Black Hawk helicopter flight was in 5 percent operational space, as it was bound for Irbil deep inside the TAOR.

■ *F-15 Flow Sheet Data*: Each fighter pilot carried a flow sheet on a kneeboard listing all of the scheduled coalition flights for the day. On April 14, 1994, there were no helicopters listed on the two F-15 pilots' flow sheets. There never was. Although the individual who filled out the F-15 flow sheets knew that the army helicopters were flying that day, helicopters were never listed on the day's flow sheets. Following is that person's testimony regarding filling out each day's flow sheet data:

> Q: Did you know that the army helicopters were flying that day?
> A: Yes, sir. I get their flight plans every day.
> Q: So, why weren't they on your flow sheet?
> A: We just don't consider helicopters to be aircraft.

F-15Cs are mainly high flyers who rarely fly close to the ground. As such, the F-15 squadron's normal work practice was not to list helicopter flights on the daily flow sheets. By comparison, the next-door F-16 squadron did list helicopter flights. In fact, on the day of the incident, the army helicopter flight was carried on the kneeboards of two F-16s that were some 10 minutes behind the two F-15s. F-16s are low flyers, so it is important that they be made aware of any scheduled low-flying aircraft. Ironically, if the F-16s had detected the low-flying Black Hawk helicopters that day instead of the F-15s, it is likely that they would have made the connection between the unidentified target and the transiting Black Hawk flight.

◾ *F-15 IFF Interrogation*: As noted in the preceding chronology, at 0723 the F-15s attempted to interrogate the unidentified targets with their Identify Friend or Foe or IFF system, first on Mode I coded 52 and then on the backup Mode IV channel. Theoretically, the Black Hawk helicopters should have been squawking via their transponders a correct signal that identified them as friendly to the interrogating F-15s. Originally, the same Mode I code was used for both Turkey and TAOR flight operations. But, out of concern for operational security, the air force began using two codes, one for inside Turkey and one for inside the TAOR. On April 14, Mode I was coded 43 for inside Turkey and coded 52 for inside the TAOR. Per flight procedures, the F-15s correctly switched Mode I codes just prior to entering the TAOR. Yet, the army helicopters did not. According to Snook (2000), no one ever told the army that there were two Mode I codes, one for inside Turkey and one for inside TAOR airspace. In point of fact, army helicopters had been flying inside the TAOR for some two years, all the time squawking the wrong Mode I code. Conversely, the failure of the IFF Mode IV interrogation could never be adequately explained or replicated. In this respect, the Mode IV failure appears to represent an anomalous malfunctioning of a technological component.

◾ *F-15 Visual Identification*: The F-15 pilots mistakenly identified the two UH-60 Black Hawk helicopters as Iraqi Hind gunships during their visual identification passes. As stated earlier, the F-15s are high flyers and the pilots had little experience flying low to the ground, especially in hazardous mountainous terrain traveling at some 450 knots with only seconds to make an accurate identification. During testimony following the event, the lead pilot confessed that he was literally "scared shitless" executing the VID pass (an obviously high stress situation). Additionally, on the day of the incident, the UH-60 Black Hawk helicopters were equipped with outriggers or external wing tanks in order to provide extra fuel for the long flight to Irbil. Mi-24 Hind helicopters also are equipped with outriggers that serve as external weapon pods. Further, during helicopter visual identification training, the F-15 pilots were *not* taught that UH-60s sometimes use external wing tanks for extended flight operations, but *were* shown images of Mi-24 Hind gunships with external weapon pods. In fact, the two F-15 pilots had reportedly never seen a Black Hawk helicopter equipped with external wing tanks prior to the incident. Nor were the pilots informed in the training session that UH-60s are painted dark green while Mi-24 Hinds are painted a tan, camouflaged color. Additionally, all helicopter images shown to the pilots during the visual identification training sessions were taken from the ground, looking up, not from above, looking down as would be observed by a plane flying *above* a target.

■ *F-15/UH-60 Communications*: The F-15s were equipped with HAVE QUICK radios that continuously jumped frequencies, thereby preventing enemy jamming. The UH-60 Black Hawks were not equipped with this latest radio technology. Consequently, the two major players—the F-15s and the Black Hawk helicopters—could not directly communicate with each other. However, both could directly communicate with the orbiting AWACS plane, albeit, in this instance, with different onboard controllers.

F-15 Pilot Analysis

In analyzing an event such as this, it is critical to better understand the incident as it unfolded through the eyes of the major participants or actors. In this case, it is particularly important to understand the event through the eyes of involved personnel onboard the orbiting AWACS plane *and* the two F-15 pilots. Here, only an analysis of possible perceptions through the eyes of the F-15 pilots is attempted, with a special focus on the F-15 lead pilot. To undertake this pilot perceptual reconstruction, parts of the previous event chronology are used as time markers. As noted previously, in such reconstruction efforts, it is important to "become one" with the actor or, in this case, the F-15 pilots, attempting to understand the evolving event through what they thought they saw and knew, and what they actually experienced, and, just as importantly, what they did not see or hear, or experienced.

> *~0500*: Pilots attend a premission intelligence briefing. Per testimony from the pilots and briefing officer, no mention of the two Black Hawk helicopters entering TAOR airspace prior to their initial morning flight was mentioned (although the briefing officer *did know* of the early morning helicopter flight). The expressed purpose of the classified intelligence briefing was to update the pilots on any potential Iraqi air threats within the TAOR region. Accordingly, the pilots left the intelligence briefing thinking that per standard air force procedure, their flight would be the first friendly flight into the TAOR that morning. It is important to remember that their assigned mission was to sanitize the area, including possessing authorization to shoot down any Iraqi aircraft encountered.

0635: F-15C pilots prepare for takeoff. No helicopter flights are listed on their kneeboard flow sheets. F-15 pilots leave Incirlik Air Base unaware of early morning army helicopter flight.

0715: F-15 lead pilot checks in with the onboard AWACS Air Command Element (ACE) prior to entering TAOR airspace, requesting "words" or any new updates. ACE replies, "Negative words," signifying no new updates. As the pilots enter TAOR airspace that morning, their under-standing—their "mental model," if you will—remains that there are no other friendly aircraft in the area.

0722: F-15 lead pilot notifies AWACS TAOR controller of an unidentified radar contact inside the TAOR that represents a low-flying, slow-moving target. AWACS controller responds, "Clean there," indicating no known radar contacts in the vicinity of the unidentified target. This response by the AWACS controller probably suggests to the F-15 pilots that the identified aircraft *may* be of Iraqi origin and, thus, hostile.

0723: F-15 lead pilot interrogates unidentified target with Identify Friend or Foe (IFF) system on both Mode 1 and Mode IV (the backup or safety channel). Both interrogations are negative (no friendly response). These actions probably confirm to the F-15 pilots that detected targets are Iraqi and hostile.

0725: Enroute to visual identification pass, F-15 lead reports second radar contact to AWACS TAOR controller. AWACS controller replies, "Hits there," signifying an unidentified contact is now displayed on the controller's screen as well. A response of "paint there" or "green there" would have signified to the F-15 pilots that the contacts were friendly. "Hits there," however, signifies that the radar contact is still "unidentified." This exchange with the AWACS controller probably fur-ther reinforced the perception that identified contacts are Iraqi hostiles and *not* friendlies.

0728: F-15 lead pilot has a "visual" sighting at five nautical miles and closes in to pass above and behind the target that is flying approxi-mately 200 feet above the ground. F-15 lead pilot flies at some 500 feet above the target and 1,000 feet off to the target's right. F-15 lead reports, "Tally two Hinds," signifying that he has identified two Iraqi helicopter Mi-24 Hind gunships. AWACS TAOR controller replies, "Copy Hinds," acknowledging enemy aircraft identification made by F-15 lead pilot. Although the F-15 pilot is in error in this visual identification, his pre-vious training, combined with the perilous low-level flight required to perform the VID, along with having literally only a few seconds to make the identification, could certainly lead the pilot to identify the helicopters as Hind Mi-24s, a potential threat. Snook (2000) describes this visual identification task in the following manner: "Imagine trying to tell the difference between a Chrysler Caravan and a Ford Aerostar minivan as one of them passed by you going the other direction on an Interstate highway, and each of you were driving in excess of 150 mph, and your two lanes were separated by at least three football fields, and the only view you had of the vans was from above and behind and the vans were painted with appropriate camouflage paint, ... and you had a mountain staring you in the face. ..."

0728.5: F-15 wing or second pilot conducts independent VID and calls, "Tally Two." This response seems to confirm to the F-15 lead pilot that his wingman also saw, identified, and visually confirmed, that the two low-flying aircraft were Iraqi Hind M-24 helicopters. Yet, somewhat ironically, in later testimony, the second pilot noted, "I never came out and said that they ... positively ID'd as Hinds. I came in on that ID pass; I saw the high engines, the sloping wings, the camouflaged body, no fin flashings or markings, I pulled off left, I called, 'Tally two.' I did not identify them as hostile; I did not identify them as friendly. I expected to see Hinds on the call my flight leader had made. I didn't see anything that disputed that." Imagine, for example, that you and a friend are driving down the road and you point out that "there are two deer on the side of the road," and your friend acknowledges the sighting with "tally two." Wouldn't you believe that she was acknowledging and agreeing with your previous "two deer" sighting?

0729: F-15 lead calls AWACS controller and reports: "Cougar (AWACS call sign), Tiger 02 (call sign for F-15 wing pilot) has tallied two Hinds, engaged." Note AWACS controller does not call off pending attack. Once again, a lack of a countercommand from the AWACS controller probably continues to confirm to the lead pilot that the two identified aircraft are hostile Iraqi helicopters.

0729: F-15 lead pilot orders targeting and instructs his wing pilot to "arm hot." He further executes a final Mode I IFF check, but once again receives a negative response, only reinforcing the perception that he is dealing with hostile Iraqi aircraft.

Note how, throughout this entire temporal sequence, at least from the lead pilot's perspective, that there is nothing to indicate that the observed aircraft are friendly U.S. Army helicopters. That is, the pilot's understanding was:

▪ His flight was the first friendly aircraft flight into the TAOR that morning; he was unaware of the helicopter flight.
▪ Radar contacts were not confirmed to be friendly by the onboard AWACS controller, only as "unidentified."
▪ Identify Friend or Foe responses were all negative. A "positive" response would indicate friendly aircraft.
▪ Visual identification passes fit outline of Iraqi Hind Mi-24 helicopters. In fact, after seeing the helicopters during the visual identification flight, the F-15 lead pilot testified that he, "… had no doubt it was a Hind. My only question was did I mix up the wording between Hind and Hip? So, I checked my book to make sure. But, basically with the sponsons and the tail section of the aircraft, I was definite, it was a Hind."
▪ Lead pilot's wingman seems to confirm this Iraqi Hind helicopter identification with "Tally two" call after his own visual identification pass.
▪ Just prior to missile launch, AWACS controller does not cancel attack. Additionally, final Friend or Foe query remains negative.

Perhaps most important of all, in this whole event sequence, no one ever said *specifically* that those helicopters were friendly—not the briefing intelligence officer, not the person filling out the list of flights on the kneeboards, not ACE or the TAOR controller onboard the AWACS plane, or their own Mode I and Mode IV IFF interrogation systems. Thus, from the perspective of being one with the lead pilot, it seems that his actions are justified, albeit, mistakenly, and tragically so.

Although the two F-15 pilots did violate the altitude restriction of flying below 10,000 feet without permission, their mission, as previously stated, was to sanitize the area, including possessing the authorization to shoot down any Iraqi aircraft encountered *prior* to the day's subsequent scheduled coalition flights.

In many ways, this incident, at least for the involved F-15 pilots, is similar to my nuclear power plant control room example described in Chapter 4. In that example, control room personnel were essentially set up to fail. A similar "set-up" situation is also evidenced here, although admittedly, the pilots failed to properly identify the helicopters as friendly U.S. Army Black Hawks during their visual identification passes. However, in a later reenactment of those earlier visual identification passes by the two F-15 aircraft, it was determined that such a correct visual identification would have been extremely difficult to make, especially given the position of the helicopters in relation to the passing jet fighters and the mountainous terrain facing the pilots that morning.

After investigating the incident, the air force initially did not find the pilots directly responsible for the tragedy. However, after mounting political pressure was applied for some form of "action," the pilots were subsequently punished. Both pilots were disqualified from flying for three years, essentially ending their military careers.

Additionally, the AWACS senior director was subject to a court martial, but subsequently found innocent. However, he was disqualified from air operations for three years. The AWACS enroute controller also was disqualified from air operations for three years. Finally, the AWACS TAOR controller could not be assigned duties involving the control of aircraft for three years. Like the pilots, these punishments essentially ended the involved AWACS members' military careers.

As perhaps an insightful side note, I have presented this case study to some 370 managers during a number of safety-related leadership training courses at a large federal government facility. At the end of each presentation, I divided the training class into small groups and asked them whether the two F-15 pilots should be court-martialed. Out of 28 different groups assigned this task, 11 groups (or some 36 percent) thought the F-15 lead pilot should be court-martialed. Additionally, 12 groups thought the F-15 wingman should be court-martialed. Perhaps Gawande (2009) was correct when he noted that failures of "… ignorance we commonly forgive. Failures of ineptitude we commonly don't forgive," even when that ineptitude may be brought on by systemic organizational weaknesses occurring under just the exact right conditions.

Note once again the "methodology" for analyzing this friendly fire event. I first gathered some general background information, thus setting the initial incident scene. Next, I developed a detailed "just the facts" timeline or chronology of the event. I further added some "meat" to this constructed chronology by identifying various compounding factors, many of them representing latent factors that made the system highly vulnerable to failure and helped set up the two F-15 pilots to fail. Finally, I attempted to reconstruct the incident from the perspective of the two F-15 pilots themselves, especially the F-15 lead pilot who was one of the "main" actors in this incident. My goal in this F-15 pilot reconstruction was to view the incident from the inside looking out, not from the outside looking in or with biased hindsight.

Note that, by adopting this "inside out" perspective, the F-15 lead pilot's behavior appears rational, albeit, erroneous. Yet, even with this "inside out" perspective and discovered insights, it is sometimes difficult if not impossible to simply blame context or "right" conditions and systemic organizational weaknesses for a tragedy. Often, as this case study illustrates, pressure is mounted to place human blame, requiring some form of punishment or legal action.

Hopefully this "big accident" case study, although certainly disturbing, provides some indication of how to go about analyzing and investigating this thing we call "human error" from the inside looking out. The same type of analysis can be applied in better understanding quality-related problems as well. For example, one major pharmaceutical company has suffered a number of drug-related quality problems, ranging from metal shavings found in a drug to incorrect levels of an active ingredient to bad odors. Some or all of these problems probably involved human error. Understanding those errors from the perspective of the "error maker" should be an important part of any quality problem-focused internal investigation.

Additionally, whenever I am performing a human error-related analysis, I like to have a series of generic "pointer" questions to continuously refer to, all safely housed in my back pocket. The developed question set delves deeper into the perception–cognition–action or PCA cycle as described in Chapter 3.

Further PCA Cycle Inquiries

In most instances, and as previously noted, human error at the individual level involves some problem of perception, cognition, and/or physical action. In Chapter 3, I included a few initial questions that one can use to begin investigating the PCA cycle at this individual human level. I also have an expanded list that is presented here. Note for human error analysis purposes, I have modified the PCA cycle somewhat to entail the following five areas, each with an initial and associated high-level pointer question:

1. *Input detection* (of a stimulus or sensory input). Was an input initially detected, sensed, or perceived? Note that as used here, input detection does not imply that it also was understood, but only that it was perceived or in some way sensed.
2. *Input understanding.* Was the meaning and implications of the detected input correctly and completely understood or known?

3. *Action selection* (based on input understanding). Was an appropriate action selected given initial input understanding and the specific circumstances of the event or task.
4. *Action planning* (based on selected action). Was an appropriate plan developed to execute the required action(s) that was previously selected?
5. *Action execution.* Finally, was a correct action initiated and physically sustained for successful task completion?

Depending on what I discover in this initial question set, I also have a lower-level list of more pointed questions. For all recorded "no" answers, I then delve deeper to try to better understand the specifics of the identified problem area. This list includes the following 15 queries.

1. Attention: Did personnel appear to be attending to the input at the time of its presentation?
2. Input discrimination: Could input be adequately discriminated from other, possibly similar inputs? Were signal-to-noise ratios and associated displays adequate for input discrimination?
3. Input recognition: Did personnel correctly recognize or identify the presented input?
4. Explanation generation: Were various and plausible explanations generated to explain input meaning?
5. Explanation evaluation: Were generated explanations adequately evaluated?
6. Explanation selection: Given the circumstances at time of input understanding, was an acceptable explanation for the detected input selected?
7. Generation of action options: Were multiple, plausible action options generated?
8. Action option evaluation: Were the generated action options and their possible consequences adequately evaluated?
9. Action selection: Given the circumstances at time of action selection, was an acceptable action selected?
10. Identification and understanding of required action steps and step sequence: Were steps and step sequence associated with the selected action adequately identified and understood?
11. Identification of required resources: Were resources required to execute the selected action adequately identified?
12. Procurement of resources: Were the required resources adequately procured and available (within easy access) before initiating the selected actions?

13. Initiation of action: Was the selected action successfully initiated (i.e., started)?
14. Sustainment of action: Was the action sustained long enough to successfully complete all required tasks?
15. Action control: During execution of the action, were adequate controls and adjustments made to ensure successful execution and completion of the task (e.g., no errors of omission or commission were made)?

I have found this second, lower-level list to be extremely valuable. For example, in the above friendly fire incident, pilot-focused questions regarding *explanation generation, explanation evaluation,* and *explanation selection* would be especially important questions to begin to explore. Or, more specifically, why didn't the two F-15 pilots consider that the unidentified aircraft may have been friendly aircraft? Or, in point of fact, did they consider this alternative explanation, but subsequently discarded it? And, if they did discard this alternative explanation, then why? These explanation-related questions would certainly be in my million-dollar question set, as described earlier.

I often will use some of these questions while interviewing personnel involved in an incident. However, when I do use them, I always first "translate" a question in such a way that an individual can better understand it. For example, I would never ask someone if an input could be adequately discriminated from other, possibly similar inputs. Nor would I ask if signal-to-noise ratios and associated displays were adequate for input discrimination. Instead, I would ask if control room displays allowed personnel to easily and accurately determine if a specific valve was completely closed or still partially opened.

My own personal experience in conducting accident investigations is that they can sometimes be quite stressful for onsite investigators. Under such stressful conditions, it is easy to overlook something that could be of critical importance later. By carrying already prepared "pointer" questions, such as the ones presented here, one can often avoid the postinvestigation "I should have asked that question" or "I should have investigated that area" quandaries.

Remember, methodology counts. By using the prescribed PCA framework as described here, one can assess human performance and associated human error in a more systematic manner that will hopefully provide insights into why someone's assessments and actions made sense to them at the time of the incident.

In summary, a systematic and objective human error-related inquiry into an incident, irrespective of type, can often provide valuable clues into why someone's behavior appeared rational to that person at the time of the incident, if possibly erroneous. The key to garnering such insights, however, is to always view an incident from the inside looking out, and not from the outside looking in or retrospectively.

A nuclear power control room operator once told me following an incident that all he has is "… his instruments" or displays in the control room. Thus, the critical question to ask is what did he see or think he saw on those instruments during the actual incident? Not what some people might think that he should have seen and should have known.

Chapter 8

Human Quality and Safety Improvement

As described by Meilinger (2004) and Gawande (2009), the date was October 30, 1935. The place was Wright Air Force Field in Dayton, Ohio. And, the event, sponsored by the U.S. Army Air Corps, was a flight competition among major airplane manufacturers, all of whom were attempting to snare a lucrative contract to produce the military's next-generation, long-range bomber.

The big companies—Martin, Douglas, and Boeing—were all there, along with their proposed next-generation bomber prototypes. The competition was billed by the Army Air Corps as fair, impartial, and objective. However, almost everyone knew differently. In earlier evaluations, Boeing's aluminum alloy Model 299 prototype had trounced the competing designs of Martin and Douglas. The Boeing plane could carry five times as many bombs as the Air Corps had requested. It also could fly faster than previous bombers and almost twice as far.

And, it was big. The Boeing plane had a wingspan of 103 feet and four powerful engines instead of the normal two. One Seattle, Washington, newspaperman upon first seeing the big plane flying overhead dubbed it a "flying fortress." It was a name that would eventually stick, but not quite yet.

On that October 30th, the Boeing plane taxied to the runway, its big propellers creating a thunderous roar. It headed down the tarmac on its rollout and lifted smoothly into the air. After takeoff, it climbed sharply to 300 feet, just as it was supposed to do. But then the big plane abruptly stalled. Turning on one wing, it crashed to the ground in a fiery explosion. Of the five-man air crew, two members were killed, including the pilot, Major Ployer P. Hill.

Following the fatal and unexpected crash, an investigation was held. No mechanical causes were identified. Instead, "pilot error" was named as the causal culprit. The new Boeing plane was substantially more complex than earlier models. Due to this increased complexity, the pilot had a greater number of preflight tasks to attend to, including attending to the four massive engines, each requiring its own oil–fuel mixture, the wing flaps, the electric trim tabs that needed adjustment to maintain stability at different speeds, and the constant-speed propellers whose pitch had to be regulated with hydraulic controls.

While being preoccupied with all of these "other" tasks, Major Hill forgot to release a newly installed locking mechanism on the elevator and rudder controls. This oversight was listed as the official cause of the accident. However, some thought the real cause of the crash was that the Boeing plane was simply too technologically complex to fly. Or, as one newspaper wrote, it was "... too much airplane for one man to fly."

Following the crash of the Boeing plane, Douglas was awarded the bomber contract with its smaller and simpler design. The Douglas selection almost bankrupted Boeing. Fortunately, the army still decided to purchase a few of the Boeing planes, thereby keeping the company financially afloat. Eventually, the Model 299 would go into full production, becoming the renowned Boeing B-17 "flying fortress."

After the finding of pilot error, a group of test pilots got together and considered how such accidents might be best avoided in the future. They immediately recognized that Major Hill, an experienced and highly skilled pilot, *knew* to release the elevator and rudder control locking mechanisms prior to takeoff. He also knew *how* to do it. He had merely *forgotten* to do it.

In this case, the test pilots correctly surmised that additional training was not the solution. Instead, they came up with an ingenious and very simple approach—they created a pilot's checklist. As described by Gawande (2009), the test pilots made their checklist "... simple, brief, and to the point; short enough to fit on an index card, with step-by-step checks for takeoff, flight, landing, and taxiing."

The checklist worked. Pilots went on to fly the Boeing Model 299 a total of 1.8 million miles without a single accident. Ultimately, almost 13,000 of the militarized Boeing B-17s were built for the war effort, an incredible aviation success story.

Today, when we board a commercial jetliner and glance into the cockpit, what do we see? Pilots are using checklists to perform various flight tasks prior to push-back from the gate. In the aviation flight industry, checklists are just standard procedure, and a checklist is just one form of what Reason and Hobbs (2003) call "good reminders."

Unfortunately, many industries have still not adopted the practice of using good reminders, in whatever form. Instead, they rely on the "skill" of the craft or profession. Gawande, however, is convinced that simple checklists can go a long way in combating errors in the medical industry. That is why his book is titled *The Checklist Manifesto: How to Get Things Right.*

Yet, a checklist should not be viewed as a magical human error panacea in every situation. In fact, when it comes to dealing with human error, there really are no magical panaceas or proverbial silver bullets. However, I do believe that there are some things that companies can do that can make a significant difference.

In observing and thinking about human error over many years, I have come to view it as a three-pronged problem. The first prong is how to identify and remove latent errors already embedded in an often unsuspecting and increasingly vulnerable work system. This is basically an organizational and management issue. Using such methodologies as HEART (as described in Chapter 4) can be extremely useful in identifying and removing many latent error landmines. Because I have already plowed some of this latent error ground previously (especially in Chapter 4), it will not be repeated here.

The second prong involves enhancing perception or detection, *and* providing good reminders (which, in turn, can enhance task understanding). This second prong is more of an individual-level problem set. When I observe many human errors at the individual level, they often involve either not initially perceiving something or not remembering or recalling something (a cognition issue).

Like the earlier Boeing aviation example, the pilot of the aircraft certainly knew to release the elevator and rudder control locking mechanisms prior to takeoff. He also knew how to do it. Using Gawande's language, he simply did not get "the steps right." Accordingly, combating errors of omission and errors of commission—or getting the steps right (and remembering those steps)—encapsulates much of this second-prong focus.

The final third prong involves not so much thinking about how to reduce the occurrence of human error, but rather how to significantly reduce the actual consequences associated with such errors. This error-consequence thinking mimics, to a certain extent, a poka-yoke or mistake-proofing system as described by Shingo (1986, in an English translation edition).

In Chapter 6, I offered up my "universal motion improvement strategies" list, suggesting that it might be a decent starting point in improving human motion-related performance. I offer a similar three-pronged problem list here for improving human-related quality and safety. Admittedly, however, this list, unlike my previous motion list, is really just a preliminary start. One could certainly add a number of other, equally important, improvement strategies. However, in this introductory context, I think my short list will do. It contains four strategies:

- Identify and remove embedded latent errors and associated error-producing conditions
- Enhance perception
- Provide good reminders
- Reduce human error consequences

As noted previously, Chapter 4 addressed the first strategy of identifying and removing embedded latent errors and associated error-producing conditions. In the following sections, the remaining three strategies are addressed individually.

Enhance Perception

Picture, if you will, these two different scenarios:

- A 53-year-old man is admitted to the emergency room after complaining of severe chest pains. Immediately upon admittance, he is attached to an EKG monitor. The attending ER physician closely monitors the EKG screen, carefully observing the patient's displayed heart pattern.
- A man of similar age is driving home after work in freeway rush-hour traffic. The sun is glaring in his face, making driving conditions even worse than normal. He is talking on his cell phone as he drives. The passenger sitting next to him is also talking on his cell phone in a loud, booming voice. Over the past five minutes, the car's temperature gauge has slowly increased a few degrees in temperature.

What is the likelihood that the physician will spot any abnormalities on the EKG display screen? Probably it is very high. However, what are the chances that the busy driver in rush-hour traffic with the sun glaring in his face and while talking on his cell phone will observe the fact that his car's temperature gauge is rising ever so slightly? Probably under these circumstances, it is very low.

Accordingly, if we are to think about improving someone's ability to detect a stimulus or sensory input, then we must think about the *total* context: what tasks are being performed, where and how they are being performed, and any other annoying distractions that might be present. For, like almost everything else, context matters.

Remember once again the *Deepwater Horizon* report stating that the crew "… missed critical signs that a kick was occurring." Having previously spent time on offshore drilling rigs, I can personally attest to the fact that the "context" of a rig is more like the guy driving in freeway rush-hour traffic than the physician in ER.

I have always found that investigating perception-related issues is continually fascinating and, sometimes, even a bit entertaining. For example, I once assisted a company in helping them determine "why" workers were failing to detect critical signs that indicated an impending mechanical failure; a failure that routinely cost the company about $1 million each time that it occurred. The "critical signs" were displayed on a continuous paper chart inking out a bunch of squiggly lines.

The paper chart was housed in a large, metal box-like contraption. The top of the box had a plastic window cut into it. This window supposedly allowed workers to view the chart from above, looking straight down, but, during routine work activities, the plastic window was usually covered with a thin and almost invisible coating of oil. Additionally, *the* critical sign that workers were missing was an approximate one-eighth of an inch change in amplitude on one of the squiggly lines. And, oh yes, the box with the invisible window containing barely detectable squiggly lines was located a number of feet away from and behind the workers. Any wonder then that these signs were being continuously missed?

In another instance, I was asked to assess individual displays located on a large display panel at a manufacturing plant. To begin my assessment, I was first asked to interpret each individual display on the panel. I failed miserably at this initial interpretation task. What I thought a display meant and what it was intended to mean was almost always just the opposite. I quickly realized that whoever developed the display panel had absolutely no concept of how most humans perceptually organize stimuli into coherent groups.

For example, examine Figure 8.1. What do you see? Because we commonly group nearby objects together, most folks would say that they see three sets of two lines, not six separate lines. Now examine Figure 8.2. Normally, we also group similar shapes together. So, in Figure 8.2, most people would see the triangles and circles as vertical columns of similar shapes, not horizontal rows of dissimilar shapes, but, not so for the person who designed the display panel that I was examining. He or she would definitely see six separate lines in Figure 8.1 and three horizontal rows of dissimilar shapes in Figure 8.2.

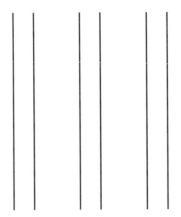

Figure 8.1 Grouping of nearby objects.

Figure 8.2 Grouping of similar objects occurring close together.

From these experiences, I have learned that dealing with issues of perception and its subsequent improvement is a bit tricky. However, it also is vitally important that we deal with these issues. Remember from Chapter 3 that if something cannot be detected or sensed, then it cannot be transmitted to the brain for subsequent processing. No mental processing further means no subsequent action can be taken, so it imperative that we get the initial perception part of the perception–cognition–action (PCA) cycle right.

To improve perception requires a holistic approach. We must not only develop better individual displays, but also create a corresponding total work context that enhances a person's ability to sense critical signals in an oftentimes signal noisy and busy work setting.

I once spent a great deal of time thinking about this "input detection" problem. At the time, I was working on developing a methodology for analyzing human-system performance in operational settings. The methodology was called HSYS (Human-SYStem). I was assisted in the content development part of the HSYS effort by Dr. Susan Hill, a wonderful colleague and personal friend. Dr. Hill and I spent a considerable amount of time thinking about all of the things that can possibly affect a human's ability to detect an external sensory input. We defined "input detection" as simply perceiving or sensing an external input. We used the term in the very restricted sense of "awareness," without the further meaning of "understanding." In our usage, an input represents a stimulus, signal, cue, or command originating in the external environment.

We next identified major factors that would make input detection LTA (less than adequate). We came up with three major influencing factors:

■ *Attention*, which is the ability to concentrate and be aware of one's surrounding environment. Attention involves two dimensions: *selectivity* and *intensity*. Attention can be directed to one or more of a number of sources of signals or to different positions in space, and may be deployed with more or less intensity.
■ *Input discrimination*, which represents the ability to detect a specific input in a "noisy" work environment (e.g., to be able to distinguish one input from another). Input discrimination may be difficult due to either a high number of presented inputs or low and "fuzzy" input clarity.
■ *Input recognition* represents the ability to identify or recognize a specific input.

Under each of the three major identified factors, we further delineated corresponding sets of subfactors. Our developed Input Detection LTA list ended up looking something like this:

- Attention LTA
  - Selected search area LTA (A selected search area is a particular position in space in which one's attention is directed or focused toward.)
    - Knowledge of proper search area LTA
    - Workplace design LTA
    - Nonessential distractions present (Nonessential distractions are distractions that are not directly related to the performance of a task.)
    - Task demands excessive
    - Personnel LTA (Primarily meaning some physiological or psychological issue, including lack of sufficient training and/ or experience. Perceptual narrowing may be especially important here.)
  - Attention intensity LTA (Attention intensity is the degree or magnitude of concentration and awareness of one's surrounding environment.)
    - Vigilance LTA (Vigilance is the process of maintaining attention to a critical input or specific aspect of an input for a sustained period of time.)
      - Task duration excessive
      - Required attention intensity excessive
      - Instrument displays LTA
    - Nonessential distractions present
    - Task demands excessive
    - Boredom
      - Workplace design LTA
      - Task/function design
      - Individual capacity LTA
      - Motivation LTA
      - Personnel selection LTA
    - Personnel LTA
- Input discrimination LTA
  - Number of inputs excessive (high signal noise)
    - Task demands excessive
    - Instrument display LTA

- – Input clarity LTA (Input clarity is the distinguishability and "recogniz-ability" of an input.)
  - Instrument resolution LTA
  - Input strength LTA
  - Instrument display LTA
- – Personnel LTA
- ■ Input recognition LTA
  - – Input not presented for detection
    - Sensor/display array not present (A sensor is a device for detecting/sensing an input. Normally, an input detected by a sensor is presented via some type of visual display, annunciator, or audible alarm. An annunciator is a display that has an audible indication as well as a visible one.)
    - Sensor/display location
    - Sensor/display malfunction
    - Sensor detection level LTA
  - – Knowledge of input characteristics LTA
    - Identification of input signal characteristics LTA
    - Personnel LTA
  - – Human detection LTA
    - Human detection not possible (Beyond human sensory capabili-ties; human detection is the detection of an input by a human.)
    - Personnel LTA

What we learned from this effort is that, if we are to enhance perception, then we must create work settings that allow humans to more easily and successfully:

- ■ *Attend* to critical stimuli in an often noisy and busy work environment.
- ■ *Discriminate* between and among differing presented stimuli.
- ■ *Recognize* and identify a specific sensory input.

In summary, I think our constructed HSYS list regarding analyzing and improving input detection is still a good starting point. If we humans cannot detect or perceive something, then we normally cannot process that some-thing or act upon it in a necessary manner. Yet, in many instances, work set-tings are unintentionally created that significantly interfere with our human need to attend to, discriminate between, and recognize and identify critical sensory inputs. And, as demonstrated in the case of the offshore *Deepwater*

Horizon drilling rig, supposedly missing (i.e., not detecting) a critical signal became a prelude to disaster.

Provide Good Reminders

As illustrated in the introduction of this chapter, in many instances, people know what to do and how to do it, but they simply forget to do it. This observation is particularly true when work settings become increasingly complex, requiring an individual to perform multiple and, often, unrelated tasks. One way to combat this "forget to do something" problem is to provide a good reminder, per Reason and Hobbs (2003). As described, a checklist is one simple form of a good reminder. Good reminders, however, can take many different forms, from simple checklists printed on a single index card to advanced, computer-generated systems.

I once had the very special honor of leading a small team of incredibly talented individuals in developing a next-generation, computer-based "good reminder" system. Originally the system was developed to assist technicians dismantling nuclear weapons. We used to always say in the nuclear weapons dismantlement business that although you can have a really bad hair day, you never, ever want to have a really bad bomb day.

After initially developing the computer-based system, we tried to branch out to other settings, including aviation maintenance. Unfortunately, I think that, technologically speaking, we were a bit ahead of our time. But, with the increasing use of tablet computers, such as Apple's iPad, as will be discussed shortly, that time may have finally arrived.

However, before describing high-tech, I will explain some of the properties of simple printed checklists—the very thing that Gawande gets so excited about in combating medical errors. There are two basic types of checklists, commonly called:

■ DO-CONFIRM checklists
■ DO-READ checklists

In a DO-CONFIRM checklist, workers, either individually or as a group, perform a short task sequence from memory and experience (they "do" it). But, then they stop at predetermined checkpoints to review and physically "confirm" that a particular task sequence has been successfully completed (e.g., making certain that no errors of omission or commission have occurred).

The critical challenge in using a DO-CONFIRM checklist is ensuring that predetermined checkpoints or stopping points are the correct and physically confirmable ones. For example, if a DO-CONFIRM checklist notes to "Confirm all surgical sponges have been removed from patient" and the surgeon has already sewn the patient back up, this checkpoint obviously does little good. Although the surgical team might think or remember that they removed all surgical sponges, they cannot physically confirm that they did so. So, getting those stopping places or checkpoints just right is critical to the success of using a DO-CONFIRM checklist.

The type of checklist that I personally have had the most experience developing is called a DO-READ checklist. A DO-READ checklist is like a cake recipe in that the checklist is performed one step at a time. When you see pilots in the cockpit of a commercial jetliner performing different tasks prior to departure, they are almost always using a DO-READ checklist, executing each required step item-by-item.

Although checklists can vary in length, many are just a single page long. These one-pagers often contain only five to nine items. Why five to nine items? Remember Miller's "Law of Seven (+/−2)? The law states that we normally can only retain five to nine items in our short-term or working memory at any one time, thus, the reason why many checklists contain only five to nine steps. Additionally, the wording on a checklist should be simple and exact, using commonly accepted verbiage of a particular work setting. Also, I like to start each checklist item with an action verb (Turn, Set, Move, etc.).

I have often wondered why checklists were originally named "checklists." Pilots who first used them certainly did not check off each item with a pencil (although this simple act increases their reliability). Perhaps the reason for the name is that after reading a required item, the pilot would say "check." For example, if the co-pilot said, "Set altimeter to 2345 ground," after completing this "set" task, did the pilot simply say "check?"

According to Steve Edholm, a retired U.S. Navy Commander, that is probably not the case, however. Throughout his 25-year naval aviation career, which included making almost 1,000 successful aircraft carrier landings, Edholm cannot remember a single instance when a pilot simply said "check" after completing a required checklist item. Instead, if, for example, the co-pilot on an engine prestart checklist item read, "Gear handle down," then the pilot would confirm that the gear handle was in the "down" position by physically placing his hand on the gear handle and verbally responding, "Gear handle down" (or some facsimile of that wording).

Edholm stated that the pilot would always confirm a checklist item with his hands or eyes, and then recite back to the co-pilot essentially the same verbiage of the just read checklist item.

He further noted how naval aviators use checklists for a number of different flight-related tasks, including the initial preflight walk around, prestart, start, after start, taxi, takeoff, and after takeoff, to name just a few of these activities. Edholm heartily endorses the use of checklists and, given his amazing success as a naval aviator, such an endorsement must be taken seriously. If checklists can assist someone like Edholm in successfully, safely, and reliably launching off and landing on an aircraft carrier in the middle of the ocean almost a thousand times, then they can certainly help other crafts and professions as well.

Accordingly, using a checklist can significantly reduce the probability of making an error, especially an error of omission. Admittedly, they do not eliminate the probability of making an error, but they sure go a long way in reducing that error probability.

What makes a checklist such a powerful, yet simple aid is that it focuses our attention on recognition, as opposed to recall. *Recall* involves retrieving information from memory without the aid of sensory cues to prompt a response. In contrast, *recognition* involves only having to respond to a sensory cue or aid. For example, using a shopping list to buy groceries is much easier and less mentally demanding than trying to remember all those items to buy. In this regard, the items listed on the grocery list serve as "sensory cues." Accordingly, recognition is always better than recall. So, whenever possible, have humans "recognize" something as opposed to having them "recall" something.

Reason and Hobbs (2003), based primarily on their work in the aviation and offshore oil maintenance fields, developed an invaluable list of good reminder characteristics. According to the two authors, in order to work effectively, good reminders should satisfy all of the five conditions listed below:

1. *Conspicuous*: Attracting user attention at the critical time.
2. *Close*: Positioned as closely as possible in both time and distance to the location of the required task step.
3. *Context-sensitive*: Providing sufficient information about when and where the to-be-remembered step must be executed.
4. *Content-sensitive*: Providing sufficient information to tell the performer what has to be done, and sometimes even how to do it.

5. *Count*: Allowing the performer to "count off" the number of discrete actions or items that need to be included in the correct performance of the task step.

Identified secondary criteria of a good reminder may further include:

■ *Comprehensive*: Working effectively for a wide range of to-be-remembered steps.
■ *Compel*: Blocking further progress until a necessary task step has been completed.
■ *Confirm*: Allowing the ability to check off that the necessary steps have been carried out as planned.
■ *Convenient*: Not causing unwanted or additional problems (or unduly increasing psychological distance).
■ *Conclude*: Readily removable once the time for the action and its checking has passed.

When we developed our computer-based, good reminder system, something that we called *Interactive Electronic Procedures* or IEPs, we tried to incorporate as many of these characteristics into the system as possible. Figure 8.3 illustrates a typical IEP screen. This first view is what a technician would initially see at the *start* of an individual task step. Figure 8.4 shows the same screen as it would appear *after* the technician had completed the

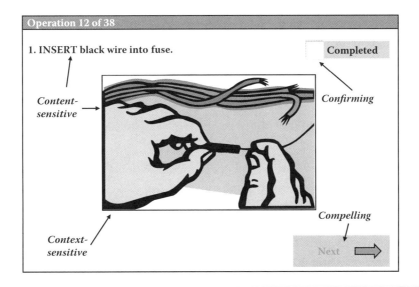

Figure 8.3 "Starting" task screen design.

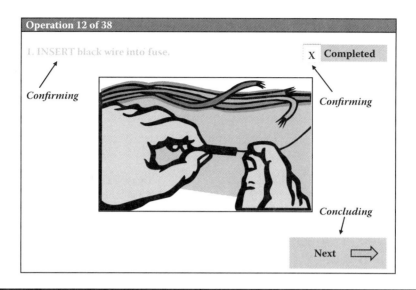

Figure 8.4 "Completed" task screen design.

task step and manually checked it as completed. (Note: The words in italics and associated arrows are for illustrative purposes only and would not have appeared on the actual IEP screen.)

Refer first to Figure 8.3. Note the task step, "INSERT black wire into fuse." The action is "insert." One object is "black wire." Another object is "fuse," which also indicates the location for the "black wire" action of insert. This task statement, beginning with the action verb "insert," is content-sensitive, providing specific "what to do" and "how to do it" task information. It is also "close" to the step needing to be performed.

The associated graphic illustrating the task step is both "content-sensitive" and "context-sensitive." In this instance, the graphic is further showing "how to do" something and "where to do it." Note also that the "operation number" on the screen (Operation 12 of 38) provides corresponding "when" this particular task step occurs in the overall task sequence (i.e., context-sensitive information). As illustrated, supplying "close" content- and context-sensitive information can greatly enhance task understanding in a good reminder system.

Next draw your attention to the bottom right-hand corner of Figure 8.3 and the "Next" button. In the actual colored screen, the next arrow is red. Also note that the word "Next" on the button is faded, indicating that the button itself is currently inactive (e.g., cannot be "clicked"). This inactive button represents a good example of the "compelling" characteristic. That is, the inactive button is physically "blocking" users from proceeding forward until they have manually checked that the task step has been completed. This latter action requires physically checking the "completed" box.

Now, turn your attention to the IEP screen in Figure 8.4. This screen occurs immediately after the user has checked the completed box. Note a number of things. First, the completed box has an "X" in it, signifying that the step has been checked as completed. This is a "confirming" characteristic, a type of feature that indicates that a task step has been completed. Also, the task step description of "INSERT black wire ..." is now muted, representing another confirming characteristic.

Finally, look at the "next" button located at the right-hand bottom of the screen. It is now active, allowing the user to move forward by clicking on the button. The arrow has also turned from red to green to further reinforce this now active button state. These next button-related changes represent the "concluding" characteristic by way of removing previous blockages once the step has been completed and physically checked as such.

Observe how we successfully converted Reason and Hobbs' good reminder characteristics into actual interactive features on a computer screen. So, why were we not successful in this endeavor? As stated, I think the main reason was display technology. The project took place when mobile technologies were still in their infancy. However, given today's rapidly advancing touchscreen tablet computer and smartphone technologies, the time for well-designed IEP-like systems may have finally arrived. Also, if one could match voice recognition with a tablet computer, it would make it even easier to use, especially in a "hands-busy" work setting.

Accordingly, I think the whole area of technologically enabled good reminders is becoming increasingly doable. For example, we have probably all encountered temporary speed sign "trailers" while driving on a local street. These types of trailers normally consist of a traditional speed sign (35 mph) and a digital display flashing our actual speed (e.g., 42 mph shown in a flashing red color). When we see these "good reminders" and realize that we are speeding, we almost always slow down, indicating the effectiveness of such devices.

Some hospitals have instituted a similar idea in their intensive care units. Upon entering an intensive care room, hospital personnel are normally required to stop and wash their hands before touching a patient. In some intensive care rooms, hospitals have installed electronic signs above the sinks. When someone first enters the room, a red "Wash Hands" sign is displayed. Once water is running from the sink, indicating hopefully that an individual is washing his/her hands, the sign turns to a green

"Hands Washed." When the door to the room moves again, the sign reverts back to a red "Wash Hands" display. Studies have shown that this type of electronic good reminder has significantly improved the incidence of hand washing among intensive care medical staff.

Additionally, on some smart tablet computer and smartphone applications, good reminders are tied to GPS (global positioning system) tracking capabilities. For example, I can put in a reminder to "buy milk and bread at Safeway store" into my smartphone. Then, when I physically drive by the Safeway store, I am alerted to "buy milk and bread," an ingenious application. This GPS-centric reminder is basically an example of the "close" characteristic of Reason and Hobbs, which states that a good reminder should be positioned as close as possible in both time and distance to the location of the required task step. In this GPS-enabled good reminder example, distance is now geospatially tied to a required task step.

With the emergence of such advancing smart technologies, we can perhaps finally begin to develop good reminders in a number of differing formats and in whole new ways. The challenge in such development efforts, however, is not just technological, rather, it also involves how to best apply sound human performance-related concepts (or good reminder characteristics) in a technologically usable manner.

However, we should certainly not think that all good reminders in the future will be technology-based. In many instances, the old standard and simple printed checklist on a single index card will continue to suffice just fine. As such, we need to select the correct good reminder format for the right task and task setting. That is, it is not about low-tech versus high-tech, but rather, it is about using the "right tech" for the right application and task setting.

Reduce Human Error Consequences

I was once asked by a company to help them deal with a potentially dangerous human error situation. The company frequently set up and moved big pieces of equipment. Part of the set-up task involved installing a critical emergency safety system. Unfortunately, one subcomponent of the safety system could be installed right-side up or wrong-side up. If installed wrong-side up, the system instantly became inoperative and could not be used in a real emergency. Although the company had attempted to paint an "up" arrow on the component, it almost instantly wore off during transport and installation. Additionally, the component was always covered with oil, further masking the arrow.

The company thought that I could perhaps design a training program or some type of good reminder job aid that would alleviate this potentially dangerous situation. After examining the problem-plagued component, I asked company representatives if it was possible to simply weld some metal plates or beads on the "wrong end" of the component in such a way that it physically could not be inserted upside-down, even if someone tried. They had never thought of this "mistake-proofing" approach before and instantly had a welder take a look at it. In the end, the welder came up with a much better remedy than what I had proposed, but the concept remained essentially the same.

In this example, what I suggested is not how to prevent the error from occurring (attempting to install the component wrong-side up), but rather how to prevent an unwanted and potentially dangerous consequence of that wrong-side up error from taking place. In essence, I had suggested a "mechanical human error consequence barrier," an admitted mouthful. We can apply this same human error barrier concept in essentially any work setting, focusing on reducing and sometimes even outright eliminating error consequences, as opposed to reducing the actual error itself. In turn, these "anti" consequence-focused actions can make any system more error tolerant.

For example, I can insert a CD into my DVD player on my computer in an incorrect, upside-down position (e.g., I make a CD "transposition" error). The CD readily goes into my DVD player in this incorrect, upside-down configuration, sits there for a few seconds, and then is automatically ejected. Error 1, Consequence 0! In an ideal, error-tolerant system world, this same type of mistake-proofing would happen every time someone made an error. It would always be Error 1, Consequence 0.

Think back to Chapter 4 and my example of the Soviet-era satellite. Remember in this case that the technician transposed two numbers (a high-probability error), resulting in the satellite self-destructing. In a more error-tolerant system, the same error could have been made, but follow-on queries would have ensured that the self-destruct command was indeed the correct command intended. This type of "barrier engineering" is often termed *defense-in-depth* or *building redundancy into a system*. The goal of these engineering efforts is to make the system more robust or, as stated earlier, more error tolerant. Hard mechanical or true physical barriers are always the best types of barriers in such instances.

Unfortunately, hard mechanical controls cannot always be built into a system in every instance. Consequently, an alternative approach is to design systems in such a way that a failure can occur only if two or more errors occur in succession.

For example, and as depicted in Figure 8.5, a system-level failure occurs if a wrong valve is opened. This "opening wrong valve" situation represents essentially a *single mode* of failure. In a single mode of failure, only a single lower-level human error or component failure is required to cause the top-level failure to occur (or, in the case of Figure 8.5, the upper "system failure" box to occur).

But, now imagine that the same system-level failure can only occur if a wrong valve is opened *and* a wrong button is pushed. This dual error pathway is depicted in Figure 8.6. Note that the upside-down and enclosed U in the figure is called an "and" gate. An "and" gate signifies that the items immediately below it must *all* happen in order for the upper failure to occur. That is, for a failure to occur in Figure 8.6, the wrong valve *and* pushing the wrong button both have to occur. This "dual" redundancy reduces (but does not entirely eliminate) the *probability* of a failure.

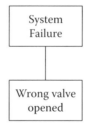

Figure 8.5   Single mode failure.

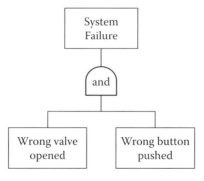

Figure 8.6   Dual failure "and" gate.

One can easily calculate such reduced error probabilities. For example, I can assign a human error probability of opening a wrong valve as being one in a hundred or 0.01. For Figure 8.5, that 0.01 number is the probability that a system-level failure will occur. I also can assign the same 0.01 probability figure for pushing the wrong button. Because both have to occur to create the failure pathway in Figure 8.6, the probability of a failure is now 0.01 times 0.01 or 0.0001 (1 in 10,000). Whenever you see an "and" gate, you just need to multiply. Note how the probability figure in this example has gone from 0.01 in Figure 8.5, to 0.0001 in Figure 8.6 by simply adding a second redundancy. Therefore, adding redundancies in a system is normally a good thing.

Astute readers, however, might be thinking back to the *MS Herald of Free Enterprise* case study described in Chapter 4. They could certainly be asking, "But wasn't there double redundancy in the bow door closure task?" The answer is yes, there was. As illustrated in Figure 8.7, for the bow doors to remain open, the assistant bosun had to fail to close the doors *and* the first officer had to fail to ensure that the bow doors were closed, all per requirement. Remember my earlier comment that redundancy reduces *but does not completely eliminate* the probability that a failure will occur. In this case, although the probability of leaving the bow doors open was certainly reduced, it was not completely eliminated. As a consequence of this unfortunate probability reality, 193 people needlessly lost their lives.

If I assume that the probability of the assistant bosun failing to close the bow doors is 0.01 and the probability of the first officer failing to properly inspect them is also 0.01, then the overall failure probability, like the example in Figure 8.6, is 0.0001 or 1 in 10,000 (0.01 × 0.01).

Now, however, let's assume that a bow door indicator light has been installed on the bridge per the captain's previous requests. Additionally, the

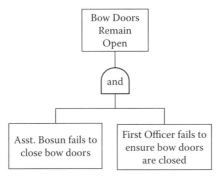

Figure 8.7 *MS Herald of Free Enterprise* **error pathway.**

assistant bosun and first officer still have to perform their assigned duties (each with an associated error probability of 0.01). Further assume that the captain failing to detect a bow door "open" indicator light is about 1 in a 1,000 or 0.001.

Based on these new probability figures, the total probability that the bow doors would remain open is now 0.01 × 0.01 × 0.001 or 0.00000000001—an astronomically low probability figure (in applied practice, failure analysts often stop at a failure probability of about 1 in 10 million). Accordingly, designing systems in such a way that multiple errors have to occur *before* a failure occurs is a valuable way in making a system more error tolerant, especially for us sometimes fallible humans.

However, note in the above examples that I used only human or active errors. How should I treat embedded latent errors in such probability calculations? I argue, and some people will disagree with me, that the probability of a latent error is either 0 or 1. That is, it is either present (a probability of 1) or absent (a probability of 0).

For example, examine Figure 8.8. Here there are five identified errors, four latent errors and one active error. Because the latent errors are already present, their probabilities are each 1.0. The active error probability is 0.01. Accordingly, the probability of a failure in the upper box is also 0.01 (1.0 × 1.0 × 1.0 × 1.0 × 0.01), or simply the probability of the active error.

Remember how I earlier observed that active errors often "trip" over embedded latent error landmines? If the landmines are already present, then the probability of one going off is essentially the probability of someone stepping on it. The same basic premise holds for latent and active errors as well.

Recall the Iraqi friendly fire incident in the previous chapter and how many latent errors were present in that system. Let us greatly simplify the

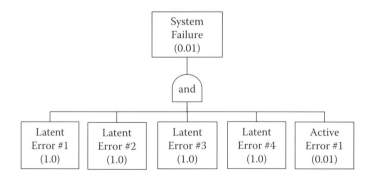

Figure 8.8 Latent and active error probabilities.

incident (an incorrect simplification I need to add) and assume that the incident that occurred on that *specific day* was caused only by the:

- army helicopters receiving an exemption to enter the TAOR prior to the morning's F-15 sweep;
- army helicopters flying to Irbil deep inside the TAOR, instead of only to Zakhu;
- army helicopters remaining under the control of the enroute controller while in the TAOR, and not under the control of the TAOR controller per procedure;
- army helicopters squawking a different Mode 1 Identify Friend or Foe code than the F-15s; and
- failure of the F-15 (or helicopter) Mode IV Identify Friend or Foe backup code.

In this overly simplified version of the incident, what is the probability of the incident occurring? Because on that particular day, the helicopters had received a special exemption to enter TAOR airspace *and* were flying to Irbil *and* were under the control of the enroute controller *and* were squawking the wrong Mode I code, the probability of their occurrence is 1.0. The only unknown probability is that of the Mode IV backup Identify Friend or Foe system being inoperable. In this scenario, that Mode IV IFF-related failure probability is *the* probability of the friendly fire incident.

That is the really bad thing about latent factors. If they are present, then their "present" probability is 1.0. Unlike a latent factor, at least with a human error, there is some probability that it *will not* happen, even if the odds are only 1 in 10. However, this human error probability "chance" factor is not evident with latent errors; it is either a zero or a one, and nothing in between. That is why the identification and removal of latent factors is so important. Depending on their type and number, they can make any work system potentially more dangerous. All that is needed in such "potentially more dangerous" instances is the right active factor to trip over the latent error(s).

In summary, reducing human error consequences is just as important as attempting to reduce the occurrence of the errors themselves. Developing strong mechanical barriers is one way to reduce an unwanted human error consequence and certainly the best way. However, another way (although admittedly not as good) is to build redundancy into a system, making it more error tolerant. Just as Thomas Gilbert thought that we can engineer worthy human performance, we must attempt as well to engineer more error-tolerant systems; systems that can absorb one or more human errors without experiencing a catastrophic failure. Or, as the old Timex watch commercial used to say, we must strive to create systems that can "… take a licking and keep on ticking."

Accordingly, reducing human error consequences, identifying and eliminating latent errors, enhancing perception, and providing good reminders in both low- and high-tech form are all good initial strategies to use while combating failure space. Such strategies can improve both the quality and reliability of a work system, and its overall operational safety.

Chapter 9

And That's It!

And that really is it! Hopefully you have enjoyed this admittedly broad introduction to the veritable alphabet soup called human performance. And hopefully, also, you have learned some things along the way, things that you can begin to apply immediately in your own work setting and associated Lean improvement efforts.

A number of key points were made in each of the preceding chapters. Following is a summative list of those critical chapter take-away points.

Chapter 1

- A work system often entails people using tools and other forms of technology to perform myriad different work-related tasks.
- Unfortunately, in our quest to improve a work system, we often focus only on the tools and/or task parts of the formula, sometimes forgetting the human element altogether.
- If, however, we are to significantly improve any work system, regardless of specific setting, then we must focus our efforts not only on all of the individual elements comprising the work system—the people, tools, and tasks—but also on the collective interactions between and among those system elements: the total work system context.
- As such, a basic underlying precept of Lean human performance improvement is that humans can never be fully divorced from the tasks they are performing or the tools they are using to perform those tasks. In many instances, it is those very same tasks and tools that are at the very root of human performance problems.

Chapter 2

■ Human performance represents a complex phenomenon involving a multitude of highly varied, interdependent, and interactive factors. Many of those factors are embedded externally in the environments in which humans work, but, some of those factors are also internal to the individual performer. Both sets of factors affect workplace performance.

■ Nature and nurture latent factors result in a unique human phenotype that, in turn, affects an individual's potential capacity to perform a given task. A particular *phenotype* defines an organism's observable trait characteristics. An individual human's phenotype results from the expression of that person's genetic makeup, as well as the influence of various environmental factors, including knowledge and skill development and prior experiences, and the interactions between these major genetic and environmental forces.

■ Natural abilities underlie skilled performance and represent the "nature" part of the nature–nurture equation. Natural abilities, in some instances, can limit potential performance levels by establishing genetically predetermined performance thresholds. By comparison, producing a desired performance result as a function of practice (and, in many instances, specialized training) represents a "nurtured" skill.

■ An individual's potential capacity to perform work is further affected by the immediate task setting in which he or she works. These task- or work setting-related factors also affect a given opportunity to perform a task. A specific task setting can either positively or negatively affect human performance. In many instances, failed human performance is more a function of a poorly designed and vulnerable work system than a supposedly fallible human performer.

■ Nature and nurture latent factors and an immediate task setting combine to result in some acceptable or unacceptable performance outcome.

■ Task analysis, task- and work-setting design, personnel selection, and training and development are all potentially important ways to improve human performance.

Chapter 3

■ At the individual task level, and irrespective of task type or setting, human performance involves varying degrees of perception, cognition, and action. This *Perception–Cognition–Action* or PCA cycle forms the basic building blocks of human performance at the immediate task level. In turn, failed human performance and associated human error often involve some failure of perception, cognition, and/or action.

- Perception represents the process of detecting, organizing, and interpreting sensory information. It enables humans to recognize meaningful objects and events in their immediate environment.
- Cognition entails all of the mental processing activities associated with thinking, knowing, reasoning, remembering, and communicating. It involves various aspects of understanding, decision making, and action planning.
- Action involves the actual physical movement of the body, such as locomotion (powered by the legs) or physical manipulation of an object (by using the hands). It represents a physical response to perception and cognition.
- Perception, cognition, and action involve sensing (resulting in perception), mental processing (resulting in cognition), and moving (resulting in action). This sensing, processing, and moving physiological and psychological model is wired together by the nervous system, which represents an integrated neural messaging or signaling subsystem.
- Sensing involves detecting an external stimulus or signal. Because humans perceive their environment (and reality) through their senses (via sight, hearing, taste, touch, and/or smell), sensing is how they actually get information into their minds to process. If something cannot be detected or sensed, then it cannot be transmitted to the brain for subsequent processing.
- Processing involves understanding, deciding, action selection, and action planning, and is frequently based on receiving a detected signal.
- The nervous system represents the body's speedy, electrochemical communication or signaling network. It consists of all of the nerve cells of the central and peripheral nervous subsystems.
- Movement is actually quite complex and involves the interaction of:
  - Bones,
  - Linked together by joints,
  - That are moved by the action of muscles,
  - Which, in turn, are fueled by oxygen-carrying red blood cells.
- If we are to better understand and improve human task performance in the workplace, then it is important to think along the lines of the Perception–Cognition–Action cycle.

■ Response time equals reaction time plus movement time. Response reactions may be either simple or choice. In some instances, response times can occur in literally a fraction of a second.

Chapter 4

■ *Success* and *failure* are emergent properties of almost any work system. As such, they may be viewed as opposite sides of the same system-related performance coin, separated sometimes by a much narrower rim or margin than we might think.

■ To begin to understand work system failure, it is imperative that we better understand the role that human performance and associated human error play in such failures.

■ One way of viewing human error is that it is a "cause" of failure.

■ There is also a new and evolving view of human error that portends that human performance is very much shaped by work system context. Within this new framework, if one is to truly understand human performance and why someone possibly performed in a certain way, then one must first understand the context in which that performance took place.

■ Sometimes under the right conditions, simple mistakes (human errors) and systemic organizational weaknesses (also called *latent factors* or *error-producing conditions*) can combine with deadly consequences.

■ Latent factors represent those setup factors present before an adverse event occurs. Latent factors induce vulnerability in a system and commonly make a system more error prone for humans.

■ Active factors are those triggering, forcing, or initiating factors. Human error is a common active factor and represents unintended actions or inactions.

■ An error of omission involves inadvertently omitting or not performing a required task (forgetting to do something for whatever reason). Errors of commission involve performing a required action incorrectly (you do it, but you do it in a wrong manner).

■ In some instances, human errors occur in a fairly predictable "place" or order in a task sequence. This observation is particularly true with certain errors of omission.

■ Basic human reliability is dependent upon the generic nature of the task being performed. Given "perfect" task conditions, a certain level of high reliability will tend to be consistently achieved within probabilistic limits.

However, given that these perfect task conditions do not exist in all circumstances, human reliability may degrade as a function of the extent to which identified error-producing conditions are present.

■ To ensure a highly reliable and safe work system context, error-producing conditions must be continuously monitored, identified, and removed. The reason for this constant vigilance requirement is that many work systems degrade over time via the introduction of potentially threatening, but often incrementally introduced error-producing conditions (and other types of latent factors). This slow drift into failure, unless proactively detected, can render almost any system vulnerable to catastrophic upset.

Chapter 5

■ If we are to think about improving human work productivity, then we must focus some of our efforts on analyzing and identifying, and then eliminating time-consuming and wasted human motions and associated individual task steps.

■ By eliminating or at least significantly reducing wasted human motions, task-related cycle times can be significantly reduced. Reducing cycle times as a consequence of eliminating wasted motions, in turn, can enable humans to perform more work in the same amount of time or perform the same amount of work in much less time.

■ Prior to performing a motion analysis, a more generic task analysis is often performed. One means of performing a task analysis is to identify all associated individual task actions, objects, resources, locations, and required specifications or performance limits.

■ A process task analysis is a type of motion analysis that focuses on human activities or what the human is doing (or not doing) while performing a task. Such analyses occur at the discrete task step level.

■ When conducting a process task analysis, one simply observes a human performing a particular task and records all discrete task steps in their sequential order. Ensuing time intervals for all individual steps also are recorded.

■ A hand micromotion or therblig analysis is a very detailed, microanalysis of individual hand motions. Therbligs are the basic building blocks of virtually all manual work that is performed at a single location. They involve both physical motions (or hand actions) and sensing/mental elements.

■ Therbligs can be divided into three types of motions.
  - *Type 1 motions* involve those motions required for performing an operational task. Type 1 motions primarily involve hand motions that pick up, use, process, combine, or otherwise manipulate an object that is essential to an operation.
  - *Type 2 motions* tend to slow down Type 1 motions and involve more thinking than doing.
  - *Type 3 motions* do not perform an operational task. These types of motions consist of activities that prevent an operation from occurring and only result in task delay.
■ Task types particularly amenable to motion analyses include short duration, discrete, highly repetitive tasks, or task sequences that are especially time-critical.

Chapter 6

■ Improving motion-related human performance often involves doing a number of small things that can accumulate over time in very big ways, particularly in terms of decreased task cycle times and associated cost savings and increases in productivity. The key in such improvements is to think "feet" and "hands." Eliminate or shorten feet steps, avoid delays, organize and redesign work settings to eliminate unnecessary search, optimize hand reach, and reduce worker fatigue. Specific motion-related improvement strategies include:
  - As much as possible, eliminate feet-related transport empty task motions. In some instances, transport empty motions are bundled with other nonvalue-adding motions. Accordingly, the whole bundle can be eliminated.
  - Shorten all transport distances. Achieving shorter transport distances can often be accomplished via identifying high-frequency transport routes and shortening those routes by redesigning the work layout.
  - Eliminate avoidable delays and minimize unavoidable delays. In relation to hand motions, short-duration avoidable delays may be caused by not knowing exactly how to use an object, especially a tool, or improperly positioning an object for a use, assemble, or disassemble motion.
  - Eliminate search and select therbligs. Thoughtful organization and associated labeling, and constancy of placement are key strategies for eliminating these two Type 2 therblig motions.

- Optimize reach. A normal hand reach is approximately 15 inches distanced from the center of the body. These 15 inches represent an immediate working space. A maximum "reachable" working space is about 25 inches in distance. Optimizing reach and eliminating search and select therbligs often go together. One enables the other, and both significantly reduce task-related cycle times.
- Eliminate fatigue-caused unscheduled rest stops. Unscheduled rest stops may suggest one of two things:
  - The person does not have the requisite physical capacity to perform the "use" motion—an individual differences issue.
  - The object or tool is poorly designed and cannot be used in a sustained manner by the average worker.

In some instances, a poorly designed tool cannot only cause fatigue and resultant unscheduled rest stops, but also may result in injury to the worker. This latter observation is especially true if tool use occurs in a highly repeated and repetitive manner over prolonged periods of time.

Chapter 7

■ In many instances following an unwanted incident or adverse event, a human performance-related human error analysis is conducted, particularly if a formal investigation of an event is launched.

■ An adverse event represents an unwanted incident with real or potential negative consequences. It refers to the spectrum of unintended and intended undesired incidents.

■ Conducting a human error analysis should consist of the following, somewhat sequential parts:
  - Obtaining some initial general background information, helping to set the stage of the incident.
  - Developing a detailed event chronology, focusing on what happened when and where, and who was specifically involved at the when and where.
  - The identification of differing confounding variables. This portion of the investigation attempts to identify all associated latent factors and related error-producing conditions that directly or indirectly may have influenced the event or negatively affected certain involved actors.
  - A re-creation of the event chronology (developed in the above second item) through the eyes of each major actor who was involved

in the incident. That is, by looking from the inside of the event outward.
- Based on all collected evidence, an interpretation of the event is finalized.

■ A systematic and objective human performance-related inquiry into an unwanted incident, irrespective of type, can often provide valuable clues into why someone's behavior appeared rational to that person at the time of the incident, if possibly erroneous. The key to garnering such insights, however, is to always view an incident from the inside looking out, and not from the outside looking in or retrospectively.

Chapter 8

■ Successfully dealing with human error-related quality and safety issues often requires a three-pronged approach.
- One prong occurs at the organizational and management level. It consists of continuously monitoring, identifying, and removing embedded system latent factors and associated error-producing conditions.
- A second prong focuses on the individual performer level. At a minimum, it should entail:
  • Enhancing perception. This perception-centric strategy includes creating work settings that allow humans to more easily and successfully:
    ■ Attend to critical stimuli in an often noisy and busy work environment.
    ■ Discriminate between and among differing presented stimuli.
    ■ Recognize or identify a specific sensory input.
  • Providing good reminders. Good reminders can vary from simple checklists to advanced computer-aided systems.
    ■ There are basically two types of checklists:
      - DO-CONFIRM and DO-READ.
    ■ Good reminders should possess the following five main characteristics:
      - *Conspicuous:* Attracting user attention at the critical time.
      - *Close:* Positioned as closely as possible in both time and distance to the location of the required task step.
      - *Context-sensitive:* Provide sufficient information about when and where the to-be-remembered step must be executed.

- *Content-sensitive:* Provide sufficient information to tell the performer what has to be done.
- *Count:* Allow the performer to "count off" the number of discrete actions or items that need to be included in the correct performance of the task step.

■ Identified secondary criteria of a good reminder may also include:

- *Comprehensive:* Working effectively for a wide range of to-be-remembered steps.
- *Compel:* Blocking further progress until a necessary task step has been completed.
- *Confirm:* Allowing the ability to check off that the necessary steps have been carried out as planned.
- *Convenient:* Not causing unwanted or additional problems.
- *Conclude:* Readily removable once the time for the action and its checking has passed.

- A final prong should be at the task design or engineering level. The goal of this third prong is to design and engineer error tolerant work systems, thus reducing the effects of resultant human error consequences. This may involve:
  - Engineering in hard mechanical barriers or controls.
  - Building redundancies into a system such that multiple errors must occur in order for a system to fail.

The role of human performance in any work setting should not be underestimated. Despite considerable technological advances, those advances still rely on us sometimes fallible, but incredibly creative humans. Better understanding and continuously improving human performance is thus a critical enabler for making work more productive, reliable, and safer.

Glossary

Abilities: Stable and enduring traits that, for the most part, are determined by a person's individual genetic makeup or genotype.

Action: The actual physical movement of the body, such as locomotion (powered by the legs) or manipulation of an object (by using the hands).

Active factor: Those triggering, forcing, or initiating factors; human error is a common active factor.

Adverse event: An unwanted incident with real or potential negative consequences; refers to the spectrum of unintended and intended undesired incidents.

Annunciator: A display that has an audible indication as well as a visual one.

Arousal: The level of action of the central nervous system.

Attention: The ability to concentrate and be aware of one's surrounding environment; attention involves two dimensions, selectivity and intensity.

Attention intensity: The degree or magnitude of concentration and awareness of one's surrounding environment.

Autonomic nervous system: A part of the peripheral nervous system that controls self-regulated actions of internal organs and glands (like the beating of the heart).

Avoidable delay: A delay or standby motion that can be completely eliminated if the right kind of change or improvement is made in a task sequence.

Barriers: Different types of measures (e.g., physical obstructions, procedures, training, etc.) used to control hazards and quality concerns.

Capability: Characteristics of people who are subject to change as a result of practice and that represent a person's potential to excel in the performance of a task.

Central nervous system: That part of the nervous system that includes the brain and spinal cord.

Choice response reaction: A type of reaction that requires the performer to make a distinct response for each class of stimuli.

Chunking: Organizing items into familiar, manageable units; it often occurs automatically.

Closed motor skill: A skill performed in an environment that is predictable or stationary; allows performers to plan their movements in advance.

Cognition: All of the mental processing activities associated with thinking, knowing, reasoning, remembering, and communicating.

Cognitive skill: A skill for which the primary determinant of success is the quality of the performer's decisions regarding what to do.

Consequence: The result of an event or action (including human error); can be either positive or negative.

Continuous skill: A skill organized in such a way that the action unfolds without a recognizable beginning or end in an ongoing and often unrecognizable fashion.

Control room: A centralized location for which operators can perform the normal control of a system or plant.

Cycle time: The amount of time required to move from one defined point in a process or task to another defined point.

Demands: Aspects of the environment or fundamental human mechanisms that place loads on human capacities for action or otherwise inhibit performance.

Detection: Perceiving or sensing some type of sensory input; used in the very narrow sense of "awareness" without the further meaning of "understanding."

Discrete skill: A skill that is organized in such a way that the action is usually brief and has a well-defined beginning and end.

Display: A device that often indicates a parameter of equipment status to a person by some perceptual mechanism; also may present other types of information as well.

Distinguishability: The characteristic of being able to distinguish or discriminate among differing items.

Distractions: That which divides attention or prevents concentration.

Emotional intelligence: The ability to perceive, understand, manage, and use emotions.

Encoding: The processing of information into the memory system.

Ergonomics: The discipline concerned with designing machines, operations, and work environments such that they match human capabilities and limitations.

Error of commission: Performing a required action incorrectly (doing something, but doing it in a wrong manner).

Error of omission: Inadvertently omitting or not performing a required task (forgetting to do something for whatever reason).

Error-producing condition: Embedded features of a work system that reduce human reliability (make it more prone to human error); a particular human-related type of latent factor.

Fatigue: Wariness or tiredness due to physical or mental exertion.

Fine motor movement: Involves the coordination and control of small muscle groups that must be tuned precisely (e.g., sewing).

Genotype: The genetic makeup of an organism; a unique and individual genetic code.

Gross motor movement: Emphasizes the control and coordination of large muscle groups in relatively forceful activities, such as in weightlifting and soccer.

Hand micromotion analysis: *See* therblig analysis.

Haptic: Relating to the sense of touch, in particular, relating to the perception and manipulation of objects using the sense of touch (particularly hand touch).

Human detection: Sensory input detection by a human.

Human error: Unintended actions or inactions.

Human performance: A human initiated or aided performance outcome, accomplishment, or result.

Human reliability: The probability that the performance of a person or group will be successful.

Ignorance: Not knowing something.

Individual differences: Differences in people's performance levels that are due largely to differences in their stable and enduring abilities.

Ineptitude: Applying "known" knowledge incorrectly.

Input: An external stimulus, signal, cue, or command.

Input clarity: The distinguishability and "recognizability" of an input.

Input detection: Physically being aware (perceiving/sensing) of an input.

Input discrimination: The ability to detect a specific input in a noisy work environment; to be able to distinguish one input from another.

Input recognition: The ability to identify (recognize) a specific input.

Instrument detection: Input detection by an instrument.

Intelligence (IQ): Mental qualities consisting of the ability to learn from experience, solve problems, and use knowledge to adapt to new situations; a function of both nature and nurture.

Intent: A psychological force to perform an act (*see also* motivation).

Inverted-U principle: Describes the relatively stable relationship between arousal level and performance.

Latent factors: Those "setup" factors present before an adverse event occurs; latent factors induce vulnerability into a system and make a system more "error prone" for humans.

Long-term memory: The relatively permanent and limitless storehouse of the memory system.

Mental demands: A type of demand placed upon an individual while performing a task requiring a certain amount of mental ability; the degree of a mental demand is a function of the task and the capabilities of the individual.

Model: A tentative description of a system that attempts to account for many of its properties.

Motion analysis: The analysis of human gross (normally using the legs) and fine (using the hands) motor movements.

Motivation: An internal need or drive that energizes and directs behavior; translates human potential into human action.

Motor neurons: Specific neurons that carry outgoing messages from the brain and spinal cord to muscles and glands via the peripheral nervous system.

Motor skill: A skill for which the primary determinant of success is the quality (and often the speed) of the physical movement that the performer produces.

Movement time: The defined time interval between the initiation and completion of a physical response.

Need: A desire for some end state.

Nervous system: The body's speedy, electrochemical communication or signaling network; the nervous system is comprised of the central nervous system and the peripheral nervous system.

Neuron: A basic nerve cell composed of a cell body with dendrites or projections that bring information to the cell body, and axons that take information away from the cell body to another neuron, gland, or muscle.

Nonessential distractions: Distractions that are not directly related to the performance of a task.

Open motor skill: A skill performed in an environment that is unpredictable or in motion; requires performers to adapt their movements in response to dynamic properties of the environment.

PCA cycle: A human performance "cycle" involving perception (P), cognition (C), and action (A).

Perception: The process of detecting, organizing, and interpreting sensory information.

Perceptual motor skill: *See* psychomotor skill.

Perceptual narrowing: The narrowing of attentional focus that occurs as a person's arousal level increases.

Performance: An outcome, accomplishment, or result.

Peripheral nervous system: That portion of the nervous system located outside of the spinal cord and brain.

Personnel selection: Involves choosing individuals for a job or to perform a specific task or function.

Phenotype: Defines an organism's observable trait characteristics, including such things as morphology (e.g., body height and mass), biochemical and physiological properties, and natural and learned behaviors.

Practice: Repeated performance or systematic exercise for the purpose of acquiring skill proficiency.

Probability: A number between 0 and 1, inclusively, that quantitatively ranks the likelihood or chance of the occurrence of a postulated event; 0 = it will never happen, 1 = it will always happen.

Process task analysis: A type of process step analysis that focuses on human activities or what the human is doing (or not doing) while performing a task.

Processing: Involves mental understanding, deciding, action selection, and action planning, and is frequently based on receiving a detected signal.

Psychological distance: All of the difficulties involved in performing a task or adopting the means necessary to reach a desired end state; the task's "hassle" factor.

Psychomotor skill: A skill having both cognitive and motor components; knowing what to do and being able to physically do it.

Reach: Making a movement or motion with one's hand and arm to touch or grasp something.

Reaction time: The ensuing time interval between the application of a stimulus and the first indication of a physical response.

Recall: Having to retrieve information from memory without the aid of sensory cues to prompt a response.

Recognition: Responding to a sensory cue or aid, without the need for recall.

Reliability: The probability of successful performance for a function.

Response time: Represents the length of time between the detection of a stimulus or sensory input and the completion of a motor response to that detected input.

Retrieval: The process of getting information out of memory storage.

Selected search area: A particular position in space in which one's attention is directed or focused toward.

Sensing: Involves detecting an external stimulus or signal.

Sensor: A device for detecting/sensing an output. Normally an input detected by a sensor is presented via some type of visual display, annunciator, or audible alarm.

Sensory memory: The immediate, very brief recording of sensory information in the memory system.

Sensory neurons: Specific neurons that carry incoming information from the sensory receptors (i.e., eyes, ears, etc.) via the peripheral nervous system to the central nervous system.

Serial skill: A type of skill organization that is characterized by several discrete actions linked together in a sequence, often with the order of the actions being crucial to performance success.

Short-term memory: Also called *working memory*, short-term memory represents "activated" memory that holds a few items briefly before the information is forgotten.

Simple response reaction: A type of reaction that requires a performer to detect only the presence of a single stimulus (e.g., detecting a "start" signal for a race).

Single point of failure: An upper-level failure caused by a single lower-level human error or component failure.

Skill: The capability of producing a desired performance result with maximum certainty, minimum energy or time, and developed as a result of practice.

Somatic nervous system: That part of the peripheral nervous system that controls voluntary movements of skeletal muscles.

Spinal tuning: Occurs when a voluntary movement signal is translated into appropriate muscle actions within the spinal cord.

Stimulus: In this usage, some type of sensory input.

Storage: The loading of information into the memory system, especially long-term memory.

Synapse: A small gap at the end of a neuron that allows information to pass from one neuron to the next. Synapses are found where nerve cells connect with other nerve cells, as well as where nerve cells connect with muscles and glands.

Task environment: The actual surroundings (physical, social, etc.) in which a task is performed.

Task sequencing: Arranging tasks in a logical manner such that related tasks are grouped together.

Therblig: Represents the basic building blocks of virtually all manual work that is performed at a single location using our hands and often our eyes; consists of a relatively few fundamental hand motions that are performed over and over again (e.g., grasp, transport loaded, release load, etc.).

Therblig analysis: A hand micromotion analysis methodology developed by Frank Gilbreth (early advocate of scientific management and a pioneer of motion study. Better known as the father and central figure of *Cheaper by the Dozen*). A "therblig" is Gilbreth spelled backwards except for the "th."

Time demands: A type of demand placed on an individual as a result of having to perform a task or execute an action within a specified time period.

Unavoidable delay: A delay caused by something for which the person performing the task is not responsible (e.g., it is beyond that person's control).

Valence: The reward value of the end state.

Vigilance: A process of maintaining attention to a critical input, specific aspects of an input, or differing inputs for a sustained period of time.

Vigilance decrement: Represents the deterioration in a person's ability to remain vigilant or alert for critical signals (inputs) over time.

Workload: The demands imposed upon the individual by the work being performed.

Zone of optimal functioning: The range of arousal levels associated with a person's maximum performance levels.

References

Barry, J. 2005. *The great influenza: The epic story of the deadliest plague in history.* New York: Penguin.

Bowden, M. 1999. *Black Hawk down.* New York: Grove Press.

Connelly, M. 2012. *The box.* New York: Little, Brown and Company.

Dekker, S. W. A. 2002. *The field guide of human error investigation.* Aldershot, U.K.: Ashgate.

Dekker, S. 2006. *The field guide to understanding human error.* Aldershot, U.K.: Ashgate.

Diehl, A. E. 2002. *Silent knights,* Washington D.C.: Brassey's Inc.

Dolnick, E. 2005. *The rescue artist.* New York: HarperCollins.

Epstein, D. 2013. *The sports gene.* New York: Penguin Group.

Fulghum, R. 2004. *All I really need to know I learned in kindergarten.* New York: Ballantine Books.

Gawande, A. 2009. *The checklist manifesto: How to get things right.* New York: Metropolitan Books.

Gilbert, T. F. 1996. *Human competence: Engineering worthy performance.* Silver Spring, MD: International Society for Performance Improvement.

Harbour, J. L. 1996. *Cycle time reduction: Designing and streamlining work for high performance.* New York: Quality Resources.

Harbour, J. L. 2009a. *The performance paradox: Understanding the real drivers that critically affect outcomes.* New York: Productivity Press.

Harbour, J. L. 2009b. *The basics of performance measurement,* 2nd ed. New York: Productivity Press.

Harbour, J. L. 2012. Understanding human performance. *Industrial Engineer* 44 (7): 26–30.

Harbour, J. L. 2013a. Home-run performance. *Industrial Engineer* 45 (7): 24–29.

Harbour, J. L. 2013b. *Performance measurement systems.* Apple iBook (can only be found on Apple's iBook application).

Harbour, J. L. 2013c. *The performance mapping and measurement handbook.* New York: Productivity Press.

Hawkins, J. (with S. Blakeslee). 2004. *On intelligence.* New York: Times Books.

Kato, K. 1991. *Productivity through motion study.* New York: Productivity Press.

Klissouras, V. 2001. The nature and nurture of human performance. *European Journal of Sports Science* 1 (2): 38–49.

Kroemer, K. H. E., K. B. Kroemer, and K. E. Kroemer-Elbert. 2000. *Ergonomics: How to design for ease and efficiency*, 2nd ed. New York: Prentice Hall.

Ladkin, P. B., and J. Stuphorn. 2003. Two causal analyses of the Black Hawk shoot down during Operation Provide Comfort. Paper presented at the *8th Australian Workshop on Safety Critical Systems and Software* (SCS '03), Adelaide, Australia.

Landro, L. 2012. Surgeons make thousands of errors. *Wall Street Journal*, December 20, A1–A2.

Leveson, N. A., P. Allen, and M. A. Storey. 2002. The analysis of a friendly fire accident using systems model of accidents. Paper presented at the *International Conference of the System Safety Society,* Denver, Colorado.

Mazzetti, M. 2013. *The way of the knife: The CIA, a secret army and a war at the ends of the Earth*. London: Penguin Books.

Meilinger, P. S. 2004. When the fortress went down. *Air Force Magazine* October: 78–82.

Myers, D. G. 2010. *Psychology*, 9th ed. New York: Worth Publishers.

Piper, J. L. 2001. *Chain of events*, Washington D.C.: Brassey's Inc.

Powers, S. K., and E. T. Howley. 2007. *Exercise physiology: Theory and application to fitness and performance*, 6th ed. New York: McGraw Hill.

Preston, D., and L. Child. 2001. *The ice limit*. New York: Grand Central Publishing.

Preston, D. and L. Child. 2014. *The Lost Island*. New York: Grand Central Publishing.

Reason, J. T. 1990. *Human error*, Cambridge, U.K.: Cambridge University Press.

Reason, J. T., and A. Hobbs. 2003. *Managing maintenance error: A practical guide*. Aldershot, U.K.: Ashgate.

Schmidt, R. A., and C. A. Wrisberg. 2004. *Motor learning and performance*, 3rd ed. Champaign, IL: Human Kinetics.

Selby, S. A., and G. Campbell. 2012. *Flawless*. New York: Sterling Publishing Co., Inc.

Shingo, S. 1986. *Zero quality control: Source inspection and the poka-yoke system*. New York: Productivity Press.

Snook, S. A. 2000. *Friendly fire*. Princeton, NJ: Princeton University Press.

Snook, S. A. 2001. Leading complex organizations: Lessons from a tragic organizational failure. Paper presented at the *Seminar on Intelligence, Command, and Control. Center for Information Policy Research*, Harvard University, Cambridge, MA.

Stalk, G., Jr. 1987. Rules of response. *Perspective Series*. The Boston Consulting Group, Inc.

Tattersall, I. 2012. *Masters of the planet*. New York: Palgrave McMillan.

U.S. General Accounting Office, Office of Special Investigations. 1997. *Operation Provide Comfort: Review of U.S. Air Force investigation of Black Hawk fratricide incident* (GAO/OSI-98-4). Washington, D.C.: U.S. Government Printing Office.

Williams, J. C. 1988. A data-based methodology for assessing and reducing human error to improve operational performance. Paper presented at the *Proceedings of IEEE 4th Conference on Human Factors in Power Plants*, Monterey, CA, June 6–9.

Yost, E. 1949. *Frank and Lillian Gilbreth: Partners for life*. New Brunswick, NJ: Rutgers University Press.

Index

About the Author

Jerry Harbour, PhD, has over three decades of technical and managerial experience in highly varied operational and research settings, including offshore oil exploration and production, underground mining, nuclear weapons maintenance and dismantlement, unmanned vehicle (air and ground) technology development, hazardous materials handling and processing, and physical security. He has managed various industry and national laboratory organizational functions, including Industrial Engineering, Performance Engineering, Human Factors Engineering, Robotic and Human Systems Engineering, Security Systems Engineering, Applied Technology Development, and Training and Development.

Dr. Harbour is the author of numerous technical journal articles and six previous books: *The Performance Mapping and Measurement Handbook, Performance Measurement Systems, The Performance Paradox, The Basics of Performance Measurement* (now in its second edition), *Cycle Time Reduction,* and *The Process Reengineering Workbook.* He holds a PhD in Applied Behavioral Studies and a BA/MS in Geology. He resides in southern Colorado on a mountain ranch with his wife.